The Anatomy of a Short Story

G.B. POOL

There is nothing tastier than a good short story.

SPYGAME Press

978-06927236-8-5- Trade

Other Books by G.B. Pool
Media Justice – First in the Gin Caulfield P.I. Series
Hedge Bet – Second Gin Caulfield P.I. Series
Damning Evidence – Third in the Gin Caulfield P.I. Series
The Johnny Casino Casebook 1 – Past Imperfect
The Johnny Casino Casebook 2 – Looking for Johnny Nobody
The Johnny Casino Casebook 3 – Just Shoot Me
From Light **To Dark**
Eddie Buick's Last Case
Enchanted – The Ring, The Rose and The Rapier
The Santa Claus Singer
Bearnard's Christmas
The Santa Claus Machine
The Odd Man - First in the SPYGAME Trilogy
Dry Bones - Second in the SPYGAME Trilogy
Star Power - Third in the SPYGAME Trilogy
Caverns

SPYGAME Press
www.gbpool.com

The interior art was obtained from IMSI's Master Clips/Master Photos Collection, 1895 Francisco Blvd. East, San Rafael, CA 94901-5506, USA. Cover art compiled by Gayle Bartos-Pool.

Summary: The Short Story is the basic foundation for any story well told. Here is a writer's guide to help you complete one.

For Writers Everywhere

Table of Contents

Introduction

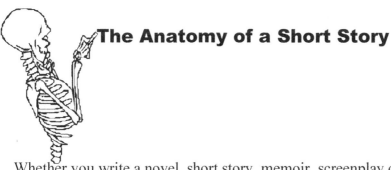

The Anatomy of a Short Story

Whether you write a novel, short story, memoir, screenplay or stage play, **you use the same basic tools.**

But where do you start?
Do you even know what type of story you want to write?

Consider your options.

What's the difference between a short story and a novel?

The Dictionary Difference between a Short Story and a Novel:
Novels are complex with ebbs and flows; Short Stories move quickly to the climax/epiphany.

A novel is like a 7-course meal going from the antipasto, to soup, to salad, to the fish course, to the main course, then fruit and cheese, and finally a flaming dessert. You are full at the end.

A short story is like an hors d'oeuvre. Each flavor is distinct, but not too much of any one thing. But you feel satisfied when you are finished and maybe you want another.

You get an **immediate effect** from a short story whereas you **experience** a novel.

A **Screenplay** or **Stage Play** can be written specifically for those two mediums or it can be an adaptation of a novel or a short story, either cut down from a novel or beefed up from a short story. And you get to add music, scenery, and physical action.

A **Memoir** is still a story. You just need to keep the fiction out.

In this workbook, I concentrate on the **Short Story** because it uses all the Basic Components of Writing in a unique way. In a Short Story you use only the most important parts. You will learn to be very selective in the words you choose, but those words and concepts can always be expanded if you want to write a longer, more detailed piece.

I use the analogy of the Short Story being like an hors d'oeuvre. Think about it.

You start with a good quality cracker. Something substantial that will hold what you put on it. That's the **PLOT**. Next you add a few pieces of smoked salmon. Those are your **CHARACTERS**. On top of that a chunk of tasty cheese. That would be the biting **DIALOGUE**. Then how about a spread of rich caviar. That's the **SETTING**. To round it out and to make it memorable, add a dollop of dill mayonnaise with a shaving of truffle. That is the **POINT** of the Story.

In a bite or two you get the best of everything.

Meaning
Setting
Dialogue
Character
Plot

I wanted to be a writer from childhood. I remember filling out one of those questionnaires as a kid that asked: What are the top three things that you want to be when you grow up? I said: writer, writer, writer.

When I was in college, I asked if I could take a Philosophy course on Aristotle. That wasn't my major, but I had a strong desire to take that class. It was the most memorable and useful class that I took during my four years of study because it made me look at writing in a different way.

I had quite a few fun jobs in my life that gave me background information for my stories, but it was that class on Aristotle that helped me on the path to becoming a *good* writer.

In his book, *The Poetics*, Aristotle said there were **FIVE BASIC ELEMENTS** in writing.

a. **Plot** is everything

b. **Character**(s)

c. **Dialogue**

d. **Setting**

e. **The Meaning/Thought** behind the story

To understand the value of **Plot/Character/Setting/Dialogue/Meaning**, watch a Classic Hollywood black & white movie. Their plots are simpler than some current books, TV shows, and movies, and sometimes better written. Unfortunately, today's screenplays fit a different mold. All you have to do is blow something up. Plots are an afterthought. (My opinion.)

I reference several movies in this workbook because the plots are almost universally known and they make for a very visual example.

Now let's dissect the Short Story. Scalpel ready. Let's go.

Where to Begin
FIRST - Get Something Down on Paper

HEAD – The Idea/Plot

Whatever that idea is in your head, write it down. Whether it's a sentence or a paragraph or a page, you have to start with something before you can begin thinking about how to make it better.

Who are the characters you want in this story? Write them down. What have these characters been doing in their lives up to the time you bring them "on stage"? Write it down.

What's the opening location? Write it down.

Worksheet #1
Where to start? Jot down those ideas you have in your head.

1._____
2._____
3._____
4._____

What do you think is the best way to open your story? You can (and will) change it a few times before you are finished. You can number the boxes in the order you want to introduce them.

Backstory..	
Character introductions..........................	
Plot Introduction................................	
The weather or location..........................	

Now let's think about that order. In the diagram below, we start with the **Backstory**, then introduce the **Characters**, throw in a large chunk of **Plot** right before the inciting **Action** sequence happens. Then add a little more **Plot**, throw in a **Reversal of Fortune** for one of the main characters that stops the forward momentum until the hero gets everybody back on track as they head for the **Conclusion**.

But as you can see in the diagram below, the front is heavily loaded with stuff and that weighs down the story. You want the weight more evenly distributed until you get near the end when the momentum is greater and there is a mad dash to the conclusion.

Backstory-Characters-Plot-Inciting Action-More Plot-Reversal-Conclusion

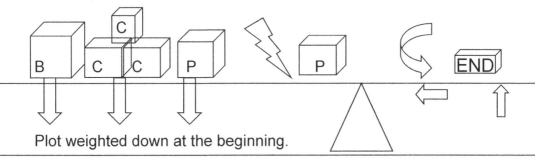

Plot weighted down at the beginning.

Here's a better way. Cut off the front part of the story. You can add bits of it later. Start right before the inciting action scene or at the inciting action scene. It brings your reader into the story faster and keeps them there until the final curtain.

Backstory-Characters-Plot
  Plot-Inciting Action-Characters-Backstory-Plot-Characters
    Reversal-Solution-End

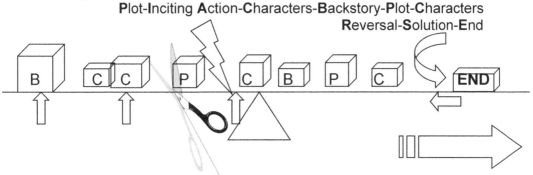

Go back to those ideas you had at the beginning of this exercise. What can you move around so you open your story at a more exciting part? Have that be your beginning. (More on this later.)

If you are still having trouble writing your story,
think of it as if you were planning a trip.
This works every time it's tried.

TRIP PLANNER

BUT REMEMBER, YOU ARE **NOT** PLANNING A WORLD TOUR. YOU KNOW, ONE OF THOSE CRUISES WHERE YOU SEE FIFTY COUNTRIES IN TWENTY DAYS. OR A JAM-PACKED TWO-WEEK VACATION OVER THE SUMMER WHERE YOU VISIT HALF THE NATIONAL PARKS IN AMERICA. CONSIDER YOUR SHORT STORY **A DAY TRIP.**

SEE 50 COUNTRIES IN 20 DAYS   2-WEEK VACATION   PLAN A DAY TRIP

On this trip you have **ONE DESTINATION...ONE OBJECTIVE...**
ONE DIRECTION that takes you to the end of the story.

    One Goal (as the titles of these movies show)
       1. Seeking a Physical Object (*Maltese Falcon*)
       2. Looking for the MacGuffin (glowing briefcase in *Pulp Fiction*)
       3. A Task (*Kill Bill*)
       4. To be at a place (*3:10 To Yuma*)
       5. Death – the Final Destination (Sydney Carton in
         A Tale of Two Cities)
      6. **A Detour** to an Alternative Destination (*Psycho*)
NOTE: In the movie *Psycho*, the woman has just stolen $40,000 and is driving to meet her lover when she comes to a detour that takes her to the Bates Motel and the shower scene where she is killed. That is where the story was really going.

Include Multiple Locations
But Only **One** Final Destination

Locations Worksheet #2 – List the stops in your story, from brief stopovers to major stays, and who is in each scene. **REMEMBER:** Somebody must learn something at every location.

Location	Characters present
1.	
2.	
3.	
4.	
5.	
6.	
7.	
8.	

HERE IS A SAMPLE FROM "JUST LIKE OLD TIMES" BY G.B. POOL
THE ENTIRE STORY IS PRINTED IN THE BACK OF THIS WORKBOOK.

1. Rusty's Diner.................Johnny gets invitation to dinner; a little of his backstory is told (*low point*)
2. Iris's house.....................Johnny meets Iris, Parker, other old actors; two gunmen barge into house and request a favor (*high*)
3. Car on street..................Johnny sees the body and is told the problem by Mike (*high point*)
4. Bonaventure restaurant......where the old actors gather to solve problem (*low point*)
5. Bonaventure hotel room......where there is a snafu and something changes (*high point*)
6. Bank in Bonaventure Hotel   where the story culminates and Vince Merrick is caught (*higher point to culmination*)

Balance out the **Highs** and **Lows** in your story. You don't want too many highs or lows in a row because either it gets boring or it becomes implausible. By breaking them up, you provide a great deal of movement.

High Action movies break this rule and are very successful, but you have to admit, the stories start sounding alike after a while. And even in a blockbuster movie they have to take a breather every now and then so the main characters can fall in love or have a laugh.

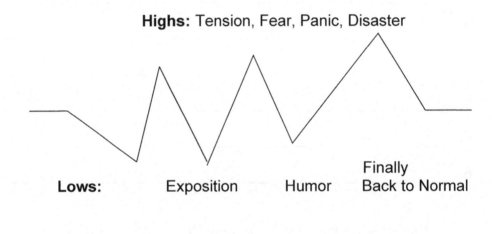

Highs: Tension, Fear, Panic, Disaster

Lows: Exposition   Humor   Finally Back to Normal

NOTE: Worksheet #2 is a basic **OUTLINE** for your story.
(And you thought you couldn't write an outline.)

Now what do you do with it?

With the last destination or goal, ask yourself **WHY** does your main character want to be there and **WHY** does the antagonist **not** want this to happen?

Many writers forget that the antagonist is really the one driving the story. If the bad guy didn't do his dastardly deed, there wouldn't be anything for the hero to overcome.

Even when there is no human antagonist, there might be a natural disaster or raging animal hunting your protagonists. As the writer of this story, you must see the driving action through the eyes of the antagonist as well as the protagonist because the antagonist's moves come first and everyone else reacts to that action.

The Why of Your Story Worksheet #3 - Describe the Why

NOTE: In "Just Like Old Times" the final destination is the hotel where the bank is and where the killer works. The good guys want to return the dead body to him.

Anatomy Lesson

Aristotle: *There are 5 Basic Elements in a story and a few other interesting parts.*

HEAD: **Plot**, Idea, Goal, Direction

Character(s) – the Heart ♥ of the Story; but with only characters, all you have is a snapshot.

Dialogue - when they talk to each other and learn things.

Structure – the Bones of the story, including Atmosphere and **Setting.**

POV – Point of View
Who is carrying the story? Through whose eyes are you seeing the story?

PACING – Fast/Slow – The Music of the story. The rhythm.

And the **Point** of the story. Never forget the Point.

1. DISSECTING PLOT–

- *"Plot is everything; the perfect plot is simple, not complex."* **Aristotle**
- Don't bite off more than you can chew.
- Tell a story that has a point, but don't overwhelm your story with stuff. If the plot is too convoluted, **write a novel.**
- Think One-Act play or TV show, not a major motion picture.
- If you get stuck for an idea, consider the "What if?" approach.
- If you get stuck in the middle of the story, try the "What if?" approach, again. (*See explanation below.*)
- Raise the tension level; it moves the story, even if it is a sub-plot.
- Keep the story moving with reversals. (*King Lear*)
- Keep the story interesting with discoveries. (*Oedipus*)
- Each reversal and discovery brings a change to the character(s).
- Hint at the conflict to come at the beginning, but don't give it all away. Even in *Sunset Blvd.*, we had to learn how/why the guy died.
- Add intensity to your story through dialogue and action; it brings movement.
- Combine elements and trim dialogue to increase the pace.
- Rearrange sections for better movement.

The **"What if?" approach** is a great way to open up your story. Maybe you have too many lows in the plot. That's when nothing happens for several chapters. That's also when some readers close the book and never pick it up again.

Look back over that list of characters you wrote up. "What if" the gal you had picked as the femme fatale, the one your detective has been chasing during three-quarters of the book, gets bumped off and somebody else is behind the major crime spree in your story? That changes everything. AND you get to write a section where your detective thinks she can't handle the job anymore. AND she has to reexamine the suspects she has left. AND she has to track down the real bad guy.

I did just that in a book (*Hedge Bet*) and it made it better because nobody saw it coming. I hadn't either until I played the "What if?" game and saw another road to take on this trip I called my story.

Since it is your story, you can do this; just make sure the road you take makes sense. If there is no reason to be there, come up with a legitimate reason for your characters to travel down it. Otherwise your readers might not want to travel with you again.

Other Ways to Keep Your Story from Flat Lining_____
MASTER MISDIRECTION

- Turn the plot around like in *Rebecca*.
- Have the reader look in one direction and the crime/action is happening somewhere else. ("In the Nick of Time")
- One character hidden in the guise of another. (*Charade*)
  > This is a great way to keep your reader guessing when you yank off the mask and reveal a character within a character with a hidden agenda.
- Hide the clue/solution in plain sight. (the stamps in *Charade*)
  > There is nothing like the protagonist and the reader hunting for a clue or a bomb or a missing person throughout the story. Keeps everybody on his or her toes.

NOTE: Going into a little more detail on this topic, let me discuss the story/movie, *Rebecca*. Widower Maxim de Winter has recently remarried a shy young woman who is overwhelmed by the constant stories about the first wife, Rebecca, from the dead woman's friends and the over-bearing housekeeper, Mrs. Danvers. The second Mrs. de Winter feels inadequate and finally there is a confrontation when she tells her husband she knows she can't hold a candle to the dead wife. Maxim turns to her and declares that he loathed his first wife because she was a hateful woman. That revelation changed everything, especially how we saw the dead wife. And it also threw suspicion on the husband and his role in the first wife's death.

In my story, "In the Nick of Time," two petty crooks rob and think they might have killed someone up at a ski lodge. They soon learn that a man has gone missing, a very wealthy man who should be wearing an expensive ring. The two crooks go back to the body, but it's gone. They see tracks to a cabin. The man is inside. The man is so grateful these two strangers came looking for him, that he gives them money. They decide to drive him back to the lodge. Once there, the man slips in the back so he can freshen up. The crooks hear from people at the lodge that the man has been found, but somewhere other than where they found their guy. The real rich guy was mugged by somebody else. The next morning a package is left under the Christmas tree. It is all the loot the real mugger had stolen from the rich guy, his ring and all. The two crooks had mugged the mugger and the mugger was so grateful he was alive, he returned the stolen goods.

YOU CAN READ THE ENTIRE STORY AT THE BACK OF THE WORKBOOK.

"In the Nick of Time" has the reader thinking they know what's happening until the rug is pulled out and another ending greats them at the conclusion. Misdirection is fun to write and great to read.

NOTE:
There is a terrific tool available on Amazon.com that you might find handy. It's called **The OBSERVATION Deck** - A Tool Kit for Writers by Naomi Epel. It is a set of flashcards that gives you hints on how to punch up your story. Everything from: STUDY A PHOTOGRAPH, ELIMINATE WORDS, RAISE THE STAKES, CREATE A CONFLICT, REARRANGE, BUILD A HISTORY, CHOOSE THE RIGHT NAME, READ ALOUD. It makes you think about your story from a different point of view.

The Logline

You have written an **OUTLINE** (Worksheet #2 on Page 15) and have discovered what your **Protagonist** (Main Character) wants and what your **Antagonist** wants. (Worksheet #3 on Page 17) Now you are close to writing a **LOGLINE** for your story.

The Logline for your story: One sentence or phrase that explains the plot.

For "Just Like Old Times" the Logline would be: *A private eye and some retired actors return a dead body to its rightful owner.*

The Logline Worksheet #4
Write a Logline: *To show that you understand your story.*

_____

_____

_____

_____

Why You Should Master the Logline

A really good reason to master the Logline is the fact that when you are trying to sell your story or novel to an agent or publisher, or pitch your movie to a producer, you might have only 30 seconds to give them the story line. The better your logline, the better your chance to sell your work.

But you need to really understand your story. You might think you know the story really well. Try telling it to someone with a stop watch set at 30 seconds. Are you still explaining the first two characters or just the location before the buzzer goes off?

You want to be able to distill your story down to a few sentences much like the brief blurb in the *TV Guide* about a movie. Read those short descriptions and see how close you can come when talking about your story. It takes work, but if you know what your story is about, you can do it.

Here are a few of assorted Blurbs/Loglines: AKA - Elevator Pitches from some of my work.

1. Johnny Casino is a retired P.I. with a past. He just hopes it doesn't catch up with him. (*The Johnny Casino Casebook 1* - Past Imperfect)

2. Johnny Casino is an ex-mobster turned private eye. He changed his name to escape his past, but what if his past was a lie? (*The Johnny Casino Casebook 2* - Looking for Johnny Nobody)

3. Johnny isn't the only one trying to bury his past. (*The Johnny Casino Casebook 3*- Just Shoot Me)

4. Racially charged Hollywood homicides bring private detective out of retirement when she ends up on a killer jury. (*Media Justice*)

5. What if a magical trip to the North Pole on Christmas Eve wasn't a dream, but part of a bigger plan? (*Bearnard's Christmas*)

6. Huge caverns are discovered near Lake Shore Drive in Chicago. What made the caverns in the first place is terrifying, but now a handful of people don't want the news to leak out and that could be a disaster. (*Caverns*)

A **Logline** gives you a taste of what is to come and hopefully a hook to grab the reader. This hook is also necessary in the **Opening** of **every story you write**.

THE OPENING LINE or PARAGRAPH or PAGE or OPENING SCENE SHOULD *HOOK* THE READER/VIEWER
(IT MIGHT BE THE ONLY THING AN AGENT READS.)

If you understand your story, you can open it with a **BANG**. And here's another little secret: the **Opening** should reflect the **Ending** of your story as well. Here are examples of some openings from a couple of my stories and a few have their closings.

1. The Opening

I couldn't believe they found Brad's body. I thought I buried him deeper.
FROM "A ROLE TO DIE FOR" BY G.B.POOL
THE ENTIRE STORY IS PRINTED IN THE BACK OF THIS WORKBOOK.

What the Opening Should Do.

- The Opening sets the **Tone,** whether it's funny, mysterious, adventure, children's lit, chick lit, or geezer lit. Don't start out funny and then turn your story into a slasher film.
- You should establish the **Genre** from the beginning.
- You might want to state the **Problem** or situation and hint at the **Solution**/outcome.

In the sample from "A Role to Die For" we get it all:
   a. dark humor; absolutely no remorse (*Tone*)
   b. probably a mystery (*Genre*)
   c. it starts in the middle of the beginning with a dead body (*Problem*)
   d. the reader will want to know if the killer gets caught (Hint at the potential *Solution*)

The Closing:

"They think an animal killed him, dug a shallow trench to hide his kill for later, and must have forgotten where it was buried." He walked closer and put his warm hand on my arm. "It was ruled…death by cougar."

Aaron smashed the plastic bag containing the vodka bottle against the fireplace and the glass shattered. Then he took my hand and led me upstairs.

I'll always wonder if he ever read that "cougar" book, but I'll never ask. Lovers have to have some secrets.

FROM "A ROLE TO DIE FOR" BY G.B. POOL
THE ENTIRE STORY IS PRINTED IN THE BACK OF THIS WORKBOOK.

First Line

2. The Opening:

"I already told you. I met the guy in a bar. We got to talking. Somehow he knew I'd been in trouble with the law before."

★★★★

The Closing:

Last Line

"Perhaps you would like to speak to a lawyer now, Mr. Harrison?" said the cop.

FROM "THE BIG PAYOFF" BY G.B. POOL

- Just like telling a joke, you want a Set-up and a Payoff in any creative writing – novel, short story, memoir or movie.

---

3. The Opening:

I always knew my past would catch up with me someday. Only thing, it turned out to be my *other* past.

FROM "PAST GRIEVANCES" BY G.B. POOL

- **Most stories don't begin at the right place. Cut to the chase.**
- Use a strong narrator's voice. (First person is always strongest.)

4. **The Opening:**

```
It was going to be the hottest damn day of the year.
Those Santa Anas were kicking up, turning the L.A.
basin into a blast furnace. If it didn't cool off,
half the state would catch fire.
```
FROM "HEAT" BY G.B. POOL

- Have a terrific setting.
- You can even start with the weather. It sets the *Tone* - Hot.
- Something is going to happen in all that heat. (*Problem*)

The Closing:

```
    I heard the front door close as I walked into the
bathroom. I didn't bother letting the shower run to
get warm. It was going to be another hot day.
Sometimes I think it's never gonna cool down. I
stepped into the cold shower and let the water run
down my back.
    "God, that feels good."
    I closed my eyes.
    All I kept thinking was, I'd really like to go
back to sleep.
    I'd like to have that dream again.
    I'd like to tell them I'm sorry.
```

- The ending of the story keeps up the heat theme.
- The conclusion says this was all a dream and the guy is still suffering because of something he did.

<u>**THE ENTIRE STORY IS PRINTED IN THE BACK OF THIS WORKBOOK.**</u>

5. **The Opening:**

It was nearly 11:00 p.m. and I was down on my knees in the frozen dessert section of the local convenience store, looking for something to eat. I had been working on a craft project at home, realized I was starving, and went searching for something exciting. That's when the sudden realization hit me that I might look like Diane Keaton in *Looking for Mr. Goodbar*, or in my case, Mr. Klondike Bar. How pathetic was that?

Fred could already be on his way home from the hockey game downtown after a beer or two with some of the investment advisers from the office. He might even be home now and wondering where the "little woman" was at that hour since I never went anywhere anymore.

To hell with the ice cream.

I started to stand and happened to catch a glimpse of myself in the frosty glass of the freezer case. My blond hair was a fright and I looked like a ghost.

Ginger Caulfield! What the hell happened to you?

As I slowly stood up, I noticed two punks at the far end of the aisle pull up their hoods and then reach under their zip-front sweat tops. They saw me a half a second later. My first instinct was to reach inside my jacket for my gun, but it wasn't there. What was I thinking? I wasn't a P.I. anymore.

FROM HEDGE BET BY G.B. POOL

- Have a **turning point** where everything goes **off the track**.
- Leave the backstory until later.
- Introduce a story-worthy problem. The beginning should hint at the conclusion.

The Closing: A Summary - In the last two pages of this book, we learn that Gin Caulfield has gotten back in the private detective business. She has done something slightly unethical to solve a crime, but the cop working with her is willing to overlook it since he, too, had screwed up by trusting the wrong people. They end the scene with Gin explaining a rather humorous incident that happened when she was on a case with the cop's girl friend. It opens and closes with a bit of humor.

A FEW MORE EXAMPLES:

First Line

> The body was beautiful, lying there on the coroner's slab, naked, except for the toe tag attached to her right foot and the small hole under the left breast. Her dark hair fanned out over the cold stainless steel in a sensuous wave.

★★★★

Last Line

> "Did you kill her?"
> Pitch nodded, and then looked over his shoulder at the young woman on the gurney. "Sandra deserved a better end to her story."

FROM "BLOODLUST" BY G.B. POOL

- The somber *Tone* says this isn't a light-hearted story.
- **Hook** the reader with a compelling reason to continue reading. In this case, the beautiful, dead body. (*Genre*)
- Even the **Title** tells you something sinister is coming your way.
- It begins and ends with a dead body, going full circle.

First Line

> There he is, the man in the dark blue suit. I knew I'd find him if I put my mind to it. It would be just like that weasel to come back to the place where it started. He just didn't know I'd come back, too. But I did. And this time I'll do something about it.

★★★★

Last Line

> I didn't bother looking over the edge. It was too dark and I had to get back. My funeral is tomorrow.

FROM "BLONDES STICK TOGETHER" BY G.B. POOL

In this story the young girl is on a mission. By the end you realize she is dead and she got the revenge she wanted.

First Line

> "But you're married, Janice."

★★★★

> The phone rang late at Norman's house. It was Detective Gomez. He had bad news.

FROM "LOOKING FOR LOVE" BY G.B. POOL

Last Line

- Establish the rules of the road for your story and don't change them.
- The beginning should hint at the ending and then come full circle. In this case Janice was fooling around at the beginning. In the end her husband gets a phone call. Bad news.

First Line

Last Line

Magic has no season, but it has many faces. And it is so much nicer when we can't explain it, because to be truly magic, it has to be seen with the heart.

****

"Why is she crying?" asked the squirrel.
"The magic of Christmas," said the large white bear as he headed for the sleigh and the long ride home.

FROM BEARNARD'S CHRISTMAS BY G.B. POOL

- The beginning and the end of the story reference the Magic of the holidays.

CHECK OUT OTHER AUTHOR'S OPENING LINES AND SEE WHAT WORKED FOR THEM.

The Opening Line/Paragraph Worksheet #5: Hint at the ending while using the *tone* and *genre* of your piece.

_____

_____

_____

_____

Reevaluating your **Opening**. If you are having trouble with your opening line or paragraph or page, think about how it ties in with your ending. (**Look at Your Outline #2 - Page 15**) Write out a sentence that captures your ending. Does it fit with your opening?

Opening & Closing Worksheet #6:

_____

_____

_____

THE BONES OF THE STORY
STRUCTURE

Have a Beginning, Middle, and End (but start in the middle of the beginning for punch)

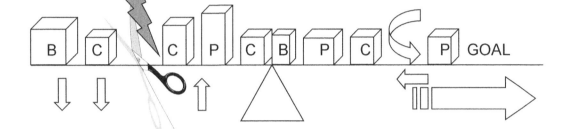

USE THE BASIC THREE ACT STRUCTURE

- o ACT I – Who is your main character? What does he want?
- o ACT II – What does he have to do to accomplish his goal? Who opposes him?
- o ACT III – What event(s) allow him to reach his goal or thwart his attempt to reach that goal?

EXAMPLE:

Act I – A young girl finds herself alone in a strange place; she meets a few characters who are willing to help her; she wants to get home.

Act II – She is told she must ask the wise man in the city that is far away for help; but someone who wants what she has doesn't want her to make it to the city.

Act III – She and her new friends have to fight their way through some tough places to get to the city and she ends up saving her friends' lives; the wise man ends up leaving without helping her; someone tells her she has the key with her all along – the ruby slippers.

This is the storyline for the *Wizard of Oz*. The basic 3-Act Structure is found in most great movies. It's simple.

29

Now for a Little Character

2000-6000 Passengers   30 People   Two-Seater

Remember, this is a **Short Story**. You don't have room for the passengers and crew from an ocean liner or even the thirty people on a bus tour in your story. Nope, you want to start out with a couple of people who can fit in a two-seater automobile. That doesn't mean you can't have somebody stuck in the trunk or maybe somebody strapped on the hood. And how about that hitchhiker. You know the one with the hockey mask and chainsaw.

Just remember, this is a short story. If the story you eventually want to write has a cast of thousands and you are really writing a novel, start here with your plot and character list to get the basic structure down. You can add to it later.

How Do You Develop Good Characters?

CHARACTERS – THE MAJOR & THE MINOR – THEY ARE THE HEART OF YOUR STORY.

- YOUR GOAL: Make your characters seem real to you as well as to your readers.
- Let your characters speak to you. You would be surprised how many writers say they sit back and let their characters talk to them while they basically take dictation. (I do it.)
- Have a reason for each character to be there.
- Combine characters to pare down the number of actors like a director does in a movie.
- Write a biography of your major characters.

HERE IS THE BIOGRAPHY I FIRST WROTE FOR THE MAIN CHARACTER IN MY JOHNNY CASINO CASEBOOK SERIES.

Character Biography – Johnny Casino

Johnny used to work for the mob on the East Coast before fleeing to L.A., he changed his identity, and started a private detective agency. He's Italian, Catholic, a loner, never seems to date except when he lusted after a mobster's wife. He grew up watching old black and white movies on a 13-inch screen and sees much of his world through a B&W lens. His snappy dialogue comes right out of an old "B" movie. His father has a shady past. He inherited lots of money and several houses from a rich client, but he prefers the cabin up in Logjam, California.

- Private detective *
- Loves old Hollywood
- A loner
- Italian/Catholic
- Used to work for the mob
- Likes women, but doesn't trust many of them
- Can be a knight in shining armor to some women
- A Black & White P.I. in a color world.

HERE IS THE PREFACE TO THE FIRST BOOK IN THE JOHNNY CASINO CASEBOOK SERIES:

My name is Johnny Casino. I'm a retired P.I. with a past. I just hope it doesn't catch up with me. Before I went legit, I ran numbers in Jersey for Big Louie "Fingers" D'Abruzzo and then busted heads in Miami for Big Eddie "Mambo" Fontaine. But at the ripe old age of twenty-four, Little Johnny beat a hasty retreat to L.A. when somebody slipped the cops a hot tip and all of a sudden, I became the fall guy for the Mob.

I opened my first detective office off Sunset three years later and tried to bury the guy I used to be. I'd catch glimpses of him in the mirror sometimes and it scared me, but it also made me work harder as a P.I. For fifteen years I occupied my time by digging around in other people's garbage. I was getting used to the smell. But thanks to a grateful client, I retired at the slightly riper age of thirty-nine.

The rich old gal who hired me wanted to know if her third husband was fooling around. He was. She changed her will, which he didn't like. She shot him five times, which he probably didn't like, either, then killed herself. I was her sole beneficiary.

A year in court with some disgruntled and disinherited relatives left me with a handsome nest egg, her big house located north of Los Feliz Boulevard in Los Angeles, and a cabin in the mountains. I rented the fancy house to a fading movie star and moved to the piney woods above L.A. to get away from it all. For the last three years I've been sitting on my butt clipping coupons and thinking my life had finally sorted itself out.

But when people get to a certain age, they change. We spend the first half of our lives trying to live, and the last half preparing to die. I had obviously reached that second stage. At forty-four, I was watching the birds and reading the obituaries...

FROM THE JOHNNY CASINO CASEBOOK 1 - PAST IMPERFECT

These are a series of short stories joined by a common theme in each book. Ray Bradbury did the same thing in *The Martian Chronicles*.

NOTE: As I wrote the Johnny Casino short stories I learned even more about the guy. Since Johnny had been a mobster, I read a book on the Mob in New York, *The Five Families*. That let me know what a guy like Johnny would have done as a mobster. I also met a retired police officer whose father had been in the Greek mafia. That man's story fit so well into the psyche of the character I was writing that I knew I was on the right track with Johnny.

Then I started on the second collection of stories and delved even deeper into Johnny's life. I "learned" something that shook up his world. It fit with his character, but even Johnny Casino didn't know this about his past until I wrote about it.

I keep a chronology of Johnny's life and all the characters who interact with him. Some of these characters make repeat appearances in the short stories. Having the chronology keeps the backstory straight.

Whether you are writing a stand-alone short story or a novel, it's always good to keep a list of personality traits, dates, and events that impact your characters. If your main character's aunt is a fiery redhead in the first part of the story, you don't want her to turn up a dumpy, middle-aged brunette at the end of the story.

Also, your description of your characters helps you see them in your mind's eye and often their physical appearance defines their personality.

Discover Your Primary Characters' Personalities by Writing a One Paragraph Biography of Each:

If you remember, we are taking a **Day Trip** with these characters who are populating our story. We only have a few people along for the ride. They are in a small car. They each have a suitcase. Not an eight piece set of matched luggage or a steamer trunk. Just an overnight case. What goes in that case?

- List various characteristics or props these people might use.
- Circle the top 3 features, then star * the most important feature. That's the thing you put in the suitcase for that trip. This can be anything from a badge because he's a cop or a giggle if she's shy; you are looking for what defines their personality.
- Keep track of hair color, height, distinguishing characteristics just like cops do when describing a felon for future use.

NOTE: When I first moved to Southern California I took acting lessons because I thought it would be a terrific way to learn about writing dialogue. My acting teacher, Rudy Solari, had us write a biography of the character we were playing so we knew who the character was right as we walked onto the stage. It was an invaluable lesson.

The Biography Worksheet #7:

_____

_____

_____

_____

Height: _____ Hair Color: _____ Age: _____

Distinguishing features: _____ Occupation _____

Developing Character

- Start with stock characters right out of Central Casting or even magazine photos.
- Pick an actor to play a character.
- What "baggage" does your character carry? Character Traits or occupation or background can define a character like Sherlock's Magnifying Glass or a king's crown.
- Understand the jargon of your character's occupation.
- Make characters sound different/quirky

What's in a Name?

Pick a **NAME** that suits each character.

Elmore Leonard's advice: *"Couldn't figure out who a character was until I changed his name, then I knew all about him."*

This goes for minor characters as well. You know what they say about acting jobs: *There are no small parts. Only small actors.*

Even an extra will do their best to capture the essence of the character they are playing. You want the guy who runs in to the diner to state that the bridge is out to have a personality. Otherwise, the other characters on the page or screen might as well get a phone call with the news.

But that character needs a name in many cases. It's true that you don't have to name everybody who walks on the stage, but when you do, pick a good one.

If the guy in overalls running in with the news about the bridge is from the backwoods, he would more likely be a Zeke rather than a Maxwell. The girl working in the dancehall would more likely be a Trixie than a Bertha. Trixie sounds lighter, almost giddy. Bertha is heavier, solid.

Another thing to think about, unless you are having fun with first names, don't have everybody's name begin with the same letter. It gets confusing for the reader.

Character Arc

At least one character needs to change by the end of your story. In a novel or screenplay, one character should have a true character arc.

So what is a **Character Arc**?

A main character goes through phases during any given story. Usually it is the protagonist, but sometimes it is a character very close to the main character. The person usually has these phases thrust upon them by nature, or willful intent by another character (antagonist), or by a fatal flaw in themselves.

Watch old movies and pick out these phases as the movie progresses. It is amazing how many screenwriters use these stages or phases. They work perfectly in a short story, too.

The Phases:

> **Orphan** – the character feels alone or is literally abandoned
> **Wanderer** – the character goes looking for clues or answers
> **Warrior** – the character decides to fight for what is right
> **Martyr** – the character risks everything for his ultimate goal

Character Arc from "A Role to Die For" – G.B.Pool

- **Orphan** – middle-aged actress starts losing roles to younger actresses
- **Wanderer** – looking for one last, great part
- **Warrior** – defends self against person who wants that part
- **Martyr** – risks getting caught and doesn't flinch when confronted

Character Arc from *The Wizard of Oz*

- **Orphan** - Dorothy is blown to Oz by the tornado
- **Wanderer** - Dorothy wanders around Oz and meets several folks who accompany her on her journey
- **Warrior** - Dorothy and her pals have to brave their way through the woods and flying monkeys to get to the Emerald City
- **Martyr** - Dorothy dispatches the evil witch and then can't catch the Professor's balloon back home. She fears she will be stranded there until she is told she has the power to go home in those ruby slippers.

Populating Your Prose

- Give each character a purpose or reason to be there.

- Make at least one character likeable or someone the reader can care about throughout the story.

- Describe characters without padding it with adverbs or adjectives. In a short story you don't have room for a lot of description, so pick a word that describes that character by giving the reader a visual treat.

Example:

He was a very big man, built like a puffy Sumo wrestler, with bulky legs more like large tree trunks.

vs.

He looked like the Hindenburg. (Or the Goodyear Blimp for those who never heard of the Hindenburg.)

Example:

The politician smiled again. In fact, he never stopped smiling. I guess that is the curse of those always in the limelight. That perpetual grin on his face was like the one a mortician stitches into a corpse for eternity.

FROM HEDGE BET – G.B. POOL

More on Character

- Show your characters in action rather than describing them down to their shorts.

  Ruby grabbed his arm and yanked him up close. "Never pull away from me. Never." She pushed him away and finished combing her newly bleached tresses. **FROM "BLOODLUST" BY G.B.POOL**

- A character too perfect, too clever, too evil, too humble, or too unhappy is too, too unbelievable.

Secondary Characters

- They bring the background to life. **Example**: regulars in a cheap dive **or** diners at the Ritz
- They provide information about the surroundings and specifics.
- They add mood and comic relief. **Example**: Joe Pesci in a Mel Gibson movie.
- They can be places the hero might not be able to be.
- They can advance the plot.
- In mysteries, Secondary Characters are called suspects or victims....

Flat vs. Round Characters (Minor Players)

Flat characters can be described in one or two sentences. They fit their surroundings and usually play smaller roles. Quite often they don't need a name because they aren't on stage or the page very long.

Example:

The butler, with the demeanor of an undertaker, escorted the police detective and the other officer to the business wing of the large house with solemnity befitting a funeral procession. It was slow and wordless, like a bizarre pantomime. The men were ushered inside the large workroom and the door firmly shut behind them.   **FROM "A PERFECT ALIBI" BY G.B. POOL**

Round characters are those who have something to say about the situation, they inform the reader and/or the main character of facts not readily available.

Example:

She stood there, all five foot-one of her, petite, platinum hair, looking up at me through glasses thicker than the bottom of a shot glass. She must have been eighty-five. Why did I seem to attract folks lingering in God's waiting room?

"You're Johnny Casino, aren't you?" she said, her faded blue eyes squinting at me, sizing me up. "You came to my house when you were looking for that dead girl, didn't you? She wasn't dead, was she?"

I managed a "no," but that was all.

"I told you I heard their voices. All those dead girls. They're still there, you know?"

I remembered her, all right. She looked like Ruth Gordon in that Clint Eastwood movie with the orangutan. Just another nutty old lady who sees things that aren't there and hears things that were never said. She swore she could feel the vibes from scores of dead girls buried in her backyard.

"Have you talked to the sheriff?" I said, resuming my quest for the perfect cold brew.

"He thinks I'm crazy." She tugged my sleeve. "But I'm not."

"We found the missing girl," I said over my shoulder. "She wasn't dead. You don't need to worry anymore."

"These girls *are* dead. I can feel it. I hear them screaming, 'Stop! Stop! You're killing me, or am I already dead?'"

FROM "THE SNUFF THAT DREAMS ARE MADE OF" BY G.B. POOL

- The fact this is an old lady is revealed one word at a time until we get to the thick glasses part.
- The old lady won't let the detective get a word in.
- The old lady gives Johnny information that he needs to solve this case.
- And she has personality up the wazoo.

Minor Character Worksheet # 8 – Describe a lumberjack or deep sea fisherman who is a minor character in a story.

_____

_____

_____

_____

NOTE: Okay, this was a trick… If you wrote out more than a word or two about either the fisherman or the lumberjack, you were working too hard. The very fact both of these occupations come with a built-in look, all you had to do was mention that occupation. Most readers will assume you mean the guy with the yellow slicker and wading boots or the big guy with the plaid shirt and an ax over his shoulder. You needn't go much further than that unless there is something unique about the guy like maybe one is three-feet tall or one had a peg leg. Stock characters are just that. A mention of what they are doing or places they frequent tells the reader all he or she needs to know. Save your word count for something important.

Without a handful of great characters, all you have is a travel guide. Readers want someone to care about and be willing to travel with, but in a short story you will have fewer people to go along for the ride.

Characters in Depth:

List All Your Characters:
- Write a One Phrase Description with the main characters at the top of the list.
- Check to see if you have too many names beginning with the same letter.
- Character interaction
  - One character is fighting with himself
  - two characters are on a teeter totter or in a boxing ring
  - three characters keep shifting allegiances
  - four main characters become cumbersome
  - if there are five or more main characters strap one on the hood and stuff the other in the trunk.

Characters Worksheet #9: LIST ALL YOUR CHARACTERS AND GIVE A DESCRIPTION OF EACH - **MAJOR** & MINOR.

Circle the first letter of the name used by each in the alphabet at the bottom of the page to make sure you don't have too many beginning with the same letter.

_____

_____

_____

_____

_____

_____

_____

A B C D E F G H I J K L M N O P Q R S T U V W X Y Z

_____

Sorority Girls Worksheet #10: Here is a fun exercise. Think about writing a story about 5 sorority girls. They are all the same age, all blonde, all taking classes. What are their **differences**? What sets them apart from each other?

1. _____

2. _____

3. _____

4. _____

5. _____

NOTE: Here are some hints: Their economic circumstances might be different. One is on a full scholarship, one is from a rich family, one is working her way through school. One may be brilliant. One not so smart. One cheats on tests. One has several boyfriends. One has none, but likes one of the other girl's boyfriends. And what if one is really a guy?

As you populate your stories, look for what sets characters apart so when you mention that character the reader knows who he/she is. By writing out their biography you have jumpstart into their personality. And make their name fit their personality.

What is another easy way to differentiate your characters?

DIALOGUE
THE WORK HORSE OF THE STORY

A character's words tell who they are and bring them to life.

GOOD DIALOGUE IS THE ILLUSION OF ACTUAL CONVERSATION.
- Get to know your characters by walking in their shoes.
- Hear what your character is saying and the meaning behind his words.

> "They've spotted mountain lions in the area and we're warning residents to watch out."
>
> "Mountain lions. How interesting."
> *And how convenient*, I thought.

(The Inner monologue in *Italics* says she now knows what to do with the body.)

FROM "A ROLE TO DIE FOR" BY G.B. POOL

- Dialogue can describe the surroundings or the weather or explain a character without using up a lot of words.

> "It's rainin' cats and dogs out there."

- Dialogue can say with passion what simple narrative can't say.

> Before Donald got out of his chair to greet me, I launched. "Are you out of your freaking mind? Marrying somebody before you even buried your wife! Do you want me to save your butt or direct traffic to your hanging?" I was speaking in a crescendo, starting around contralto, and ending somewhere in the soprano range.
> "I never loved my wife!" he declared in clear basso profundo.
> "Did you kill her?" I yelled.
> "*No!*" he shot back.

FROM HEDGE BET BY G.B. POOL

- Notice how the dialogue gets shorter as they get madder.

SOME ADDITIONAL POINTS
- Read your work aloud; let someone else read it to you; listen to your work on Simply Speaking Gold software or WORD Text to Speech. It catches things you overlook.
- Pit opposites in a scene and watch the sparks fly.
- Good dialogue is like a telegram. Every word costs you. Real speech is too long and too boooriiiing.
- Dialogue performs a function just like a costume.

The Main Purpose of Dialogue
Dialogue **enhances** (describes) the character, **advances** the plot, and **gets you up close** and personal.

o Enhances the character:

"Sweetheart, something has happened to your living room. Did you perhaps get another dog?"
                    vs.
"Honey, somethin's happened to yer living room. Did ya'll get another dawg?"
                              FROM HEDGE BET BY G.B. POOL

- Look how the accent adds to the character.

o Advances the plot:

"Why'd you get out of the fund?"
"Frankly, I was scared. They played too rough." Paul shook his head.
"**They**?" That got my attention. "Who's *they*? Does Racine have a partner?"
                              FROM HEDGE BET BY G.B. POOL
- The detective just learned something.

o Gets you up-close and personal:

I lowered my voice before asking her my next question. "Do you outrank him?"
"No, I sleep with him," Trin whispered.
                              FROM HEDGE BET BY G.B. POOL

- Simple gestures describe the character.

    "Go ahead. Date my ex-wife," he shouted.
    vs.
    "Go ahead. Date my ex-wife," he said and then slammed his fist into the wall.

- Body Language or Stage Business shows state of mind.
    "I love you," he said.
    She blew smoke in his face. "How nice."

Or how about

    "*I'm crazy about you, too,*" she said, looking at her watch.

MORE ON DIALOGUE

- Instead of a constant stream of he said/she said, show how it was said with Action Tags –

    "I loathe you," she said fiercely.
    vs.
    "I loathe you," she said, grinding her cigarette into his hand. "Have a nice day."

- Sometimes it's what you don't say.

    "I knew you wouldn't care if I dated someone else," he said. She bit her lip.

- Keep yourself out of the dialogue. (*This was Lawrence Olivier's advice to an actor.*) Don't let your thoughts get tangled with those of your characters.

- Make sure at least one person learns something during any conversation.

Recognizing Bad Dialogue
Things to Avoid

- John and Martha Syndrome -
  "John, do you know we are having company tonight?"
  "Yes, Martha. I know."
  "But, John, you're not dressed."
  "I know, Martha, but I have time."
  "But John…"

- Or *The Outlaw Josey Wales* Syndrome. In the movie the other characters mention his name about a hundred times until it was laughable.

- Adverb Addiction. "Go easy on the adverbs and adjectives," *she said gravely*.

- Expository dialogue – "As you know, Fred…" Find another way to explain things to the reader.

- The Ho-Hums – "Hello! Goodbye." Taking up space, rendering nothing.

- Perfect Grammar Problem – Get over the rules and write dialogue like a perfect swine. Your high school English teacher won't be grading your paper.

- Redundancy –
  Kathy couldn't see the boat Earl was pointing to on the water.
  "I can't see the boat you're pointing to on the water, Earl," she told him.
  vs.
  Straining her neck to see over his shoulder, she said, "I can't see the boat you're pointing to, Earl."

- Avoid long speeches, unless you're Shakespeare.

USING DIFFERENT WORDS WORKSHEET #11 – *How do I love thee, let me count the ways.*

Write two statements that say: "I love you." and "I hate you." without using the words: "love" or "hate" and avoiding using adverbs.

_____

_____

_____

_____

EXAMPLES:

"You are the earth and sun."

"I wouldn't spit on you if you were on fire."

"You are the oxygen I breathe."

As she drove the knife deep into his chest she said, "I think I can live without you, John."

We hear people talk everyday. In the line at the supermarket, at a party, at lunch with friends… unless you friends are writers, then you just might hear things said a different way. But most overheard conversation is pretty boring. Dialogue in books and in movies needs to be different. Shorter. More to the point.

Try to find different ways for your characters to say common things. It makes for a better read and it gives your characters "character." Whether it's an accent or a catch phrase that identifies that character or even a speech impediment, speech defines who the person is.

If you do use an accent, don't overwhelm the dialogue with foreign phrases. It gets old. Just a word here or there makes the point. *N'est-ce pas?*

I have read dialogue where someone lisps or stutters. It can be quite effective, but again, don't beat it to death. A few words can make all the difference you need.

SUNSET IN THE CITY, THE COUNTRY, THE OCEAN

Setting

The setting creates mood or defines a character's background whether it's done with description or the location itself setting the stage and almost becoming a character in the story.

And remember, we are writing a **Short Story**. You don't have time to visit those fifty countries in twenty days. You are taking a Day Trip. Select a few choice locations and center your story around the most interesting places.

- Set the stage with a great locale. Setting can be part of the character's challenge – Mt. Rushmore in the movie *North by Northwest* or the hurricane in the novel *Don't Stop the Carnival* by Herman Wouk.
  - Get most of your facts right about a real place you describe. The Internet is a great resource. Or library.
  - The setting can denote the background of characters from *Tobacco Road* to *Grand Hotel.*
  - The description of an area can educate, but this isn't a travel guide.
  - Too much description stops the action.
  - Characters can view the same place differently. One sees the rose bush, the other sees the wad of gum.
  - Setting can also act as a character – "Pit and the Pendulum."

- The Setting can be part of the character's challenge. Earthquakes in the movie *San Francisco*. Tornadoes, floods, the occupants of *Jurassic Park*… But in a short story THINK SMALLER.
- Think of the story as if it were a 1-act play or a TV series (the 30-minute variety).
- Create an atmosphere that breathes on its own.
  - Sight, sound, and smell can take reader away.
    Example: The smell of burned tacos filled the air while the raging surf crashed along the sun-drenched pier.

- Avoid large information dumps (character description, location sketches, or backstory) that stop the action. Show what people are doing rather than telling about it. Explain it in a way the reader doesn't perceive it to be a lecture tour.

Errors of Substance/Structure/Plot

- The Obvious Syndrome – avoid telling about ordinary events even with an extraordinary character.
- This-Sounds-Familiar – If it sounds like an old TV show, it probably was one. Avoid.
- What I Did on My Summer Vacation Syndrome – writing too much detail and no character. Readers have to care about the person (or animal) in the story, not the place so much unless it is going to be destroyed or saved.

Here are some examples that use the weather and location. The first is famous, but way too long. The second is fabulous. The third sets the stage for the story to come.

1. It was a dark and stormy night; the rain fell in torrents, except at occasional intervals, when it was checked by a violent gust of wind which swept up the streets (for it is in London that our scene lies), rattling along the house-tops, and fiercely agitating the scanty flame of the lamps that struggled against the darkness.

Edward George Bulwer-Lytton, in his story: *PAUL CLIFFORD* (1830)

2. The rain continued. It was a hard rain, a perpetual rain, a sweating and steaming rain; it was a mizzle, a downpour, a fountain, a whipping at the eyes, an undertow at the ankles; it was a rain to drown all rains and the memory of rains. It came by the pound, by the ton, it hacked at the jungle and cut the trees like scissors and shaved the grass and tunneled the soil and molted the bushes. It shrank men's hands into the hands of wrinkled apes; it rained a solid glassy rain, and it never stopped.

"The Long Rain" – from Ray Bradbury's The Illustrated Man

3. The scream echoed through the house and ricocheted off the beautifully painted walls and then bounced down the wide corridors like a rubber ball. It might have been a large house worth a sizeable fortune, but even the rich need a place to die.

"The Perfect Alibi" by G.B. Pool

POV – Point of View

- **Multiple vs. Single** – It's your story. What voice have you mastered? Which one will carry your story best? *The Woman in White* by Wilkie Collins uses multiple POVs. So does *Blood Harvest* by Brant Randall/Bruce Cook. In this case both humans and animals speak. Terrific.

- The fewer POVs, the better, though multiple POVs work if separated by chapters or paragraph breaks in a short story.

- Make it clear who's talking with tags or tone or quirks.

- The person with the strongest goal should carry any given scene in multiple POV stories.

- Don't have one character get inside another character's head.

> I saw Jane staring angrily at John, wishing she could kill him. *(How does the narrator know what Jane is thinking?)*
>
> **vs.**
>
> I saw Jane standing there, staring at John, strangling the life out of her handkerchief.

- Third Person is the most versatile.

> Sue ran to the car in a panic while Dave, with fierce determination, darted into the alley after the thief.

- Third Person Close gets inside one main character almost like First Person.

> Sue ran to the car, hoping that Dave would make it back alive.

- Don't let you, the writer, butt into the scene to explain something except in your memoir.

- Types of POV
  - First Person or "I" – Up-close and personal, but from only one viewpoint.
    Example: I had a premonition this would be the worst day of my life.

  - Third Person – the natural storytelling mode; seen from various character's vantage points; should never seem like a character itself; it reveals people's thoughts more intimately.
    Example: Sarah felt a sudden twinge, making her think this might turn out to be a bad day. She wondered if Bob saw her reaction.

- Omniscient Narrator – Lacks tension because He knows everything; great for opening a story before switching to Third Person; great for laying backstory and atmosphere, but there is no deep feeling for characters.
  Example: Unbeknownst to Sarah, this would be the worst day of her life.

POV Worksheet#12: Rewrite a paragraph from your story from Third Person to First Person or vise versa to see how it feels.

POV – First Person vs. Third Person

Archie Wright was his name. Dishing dirt was his game. His sandbox: Hollywood. The most glamorous and glitzy, vicious, and venomous playground in the world. If you come for a visit, bring your sunscreen *and* your shark repellent. If you come to stay, he'll warn you, Tinsel Town eats up and spits out a hundred just like you every day. Sometimes it isn't pretty, but it's his job to chronicle the ebb and flow of the hopeful, the helpless, and the hapless. His best stories come from the dark side of Glitzville.

vs.

Archie Wright's the name. Dishing dirt's the game. My sandbox: Hollywood. The most glamorous and glitzy, vicious, and venomous playground in the world. If you come for a visit, bring your sunscreen *and* your shark repellent. If you come to stay, let me warn you, Tinsel Town eats up and spits out a hundred just like you every day. Sometimes it isn't pretty, but it's my job to chronicle the ebb and flow of the hopeful, the helpless, and the hapless. My best stories come from the dark side of Glitzville.

FROM "GLITZVILLE" BY G.B.POOL

NOTE: I chose First Person because it gets the reader face to face with the main character as he tells his story in his own unique way.

PACING
A Combination of Elements

- *If I find my pace slowing, it is because the story is vague.* Patricia Highsmith, author of *Strangers on a Train*.

- Pacing requires Highs and Lows. Think of the comic relief in a Mel Gibson *Lethal Weapon* movie. Comedy is considered a Low to the explosions and car chases which are the Highs.

- First Person POV is the most immediate, and reaches the fastest pace. Third Person POV is viewing from a distance and often a slower pace. Third Person Close can reach a fast pace, but slightly less personal than First Person.

- Dialogue can quicken or slow down the story.
  Example: `She whispered.` **vs.** `She screamed.`

- The Setting can set the pace. `Running the rapids` **vs.** `a walk in the park.`

- Keep the reader interested by heightening the tension.
  Example: `"Don't go in the basement."`

- Different emotions can be suggested by slowing down or speeding up the action, just like the music in a horror movie.

- Pacing can be in the rhythm of speech like a detective story or the fast action in a thriller/disaster movie.

Each one of these items moves the story to its conclusion.

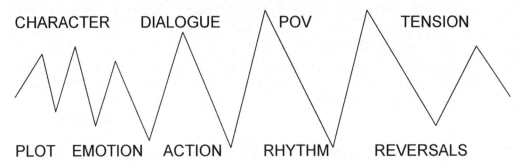

CHARACTER   DIALOGUE   POV   TENSION

PLOT   EMOTION   ACTION   RHYTHM   REVERSALS

The THOUGHT behind the Story

This is actually the most important part of your story. You need to have a **reason** to write whatever you are writing in the first place. What is the point you are trying to make?

What is the motivation for the story? What is its theme? Man against Nature; Man against Man; Man against Himself.

What is your story's purpose? Religious, political, humorous anecdote, a true love story; crime doesn't pay?

To see if you have a point:

- **Write a Logline** for your story and discover what story you are trying to tell. It's all there in your **Plot**.

- If you don't know what your story is about, nobody else will either. Think about it.

- Write a **Character(s)** people will care about.

- Give your characters a Voice by using **Dialogue** that tells the story you want to tell.

- Pick a memorable **Setting** that fits your story.

Wrap Up

Write the story you want to write. Remember Aristotle's advice about the **Five Elements** in a story. If the PLOT is solid, the CHARACTERS memorable, the SETTING interesting, the DIALOGUE realistic, and there is a POINT to your tale, you'll have written a pretty darn good story.

One Last Thing

When I teach this class I use a lot of props. I have a life-size Styrofoam skeleton that is spread out on a table. After all, I call it The Anatomy of a Short Story. As I go through the "anatomy lesson," I point to the skull to represent plot, the heart to signify the characters, and the feet symbolize the story's pacing. I have a pair of glasses that represents POV.

By the time I am finished with the class, I have used all the props… except one. Sitting on the table is also a large black crow. He sits there all through the lesson. I ask my students if there is anything I have forgotten and there will always be someone who points to the crow. Throughout the class, I never mentioned the black bird.

That's when I bring up **Chekhov's Gun**. Anton Chekhov was a Russian playwright and short story writer. His works *The Cherry Orchard* and *Uncle Vanya* are classics. He is considered one of the greatest short story writers in history. He is second to Shakespeare in popularity among writers of all genres.

When explaining how to write a story Chekhov said:

Remove everything that has no relevance to the story. If you say in the first chapter that there is a rifle hanging on the wall, in the second or third chapter it absolutely must go off. If it's not going to be fired, it shouldn't be hanging there. **Anton Chekhov**

Here's my take: When you are writing your story, go through all the sections (Look at your Outline.) and see if you have mentioned something or someone (Look at your list of characters.) that makes absolutely no contribution to the story. If you find something that has no purpose, take it out or write something in the conclusion that utilizes that thing or person. It's fair to your readers and it shows you have been thinking while writing your story.

Stuff to Remember

- All Rules Can Be Broken.
- If it doesn't work, go back to the Rules.
- It's your story, write it the way you want it.
- If it still doesn't work, go back to the Rules.
- Great writers didn't follow rules; they wrote them. Who taught Aristotle?
- But then again, Aristotle wrote some rules.
- It's always best to love what you write; but you might be the only one who does.
- So if all else fails, go back to the Rules.
- Best of luck to you all.

G.B.Pool

Marketing Your Story

The Short Story Market isn't robust at the time of this publication. There are still contests and anthologies that do a fine job of showcasing writers - new and old. Join writers' clubs that publish an anthology annually or bi-annually. On-line writers' sites pop up every now and then that publish short stories. Many don't pay anything, but you still might get your work in print, so ask fellow writers if they know of any opportunities and search the Internet for places that take short stories.

Something else to think about: Save those short stories that don't make it into a published anthology and self-publish a collection of your own stories. Whether a mixed collection or joined stories, you might be able to turn them into a book.

Magazines and E-zines that Take Short Stories

    a. www.GlimmerTrainPress.com
    b. Zeotrope at www.all-story.com
    c. www.Boulevardmagazine.org
    d. Cimarron Review @ http://cimarronreview.okstate.edu
    e. *Ellery Queen Mystery Magazine*
    http://www.themysteryplace.com/eqmm/guidelines/
    f. *Alfred Hitchcock Magazine*
    http://www.themysteryplace.com/ahmm/guidelines
    g. Chicken Soup for the Soul Series – www.chickensoup.com
    h. *Reader's Digest* – www.rd.com and go to Contact Us

E-Zines that Might Publish Your Work

    a. www.Everydayfiction.com
    b. Kings River Life Magazine – www.kingsriverlife.com
    c. www.heliotropemag.com

►A good reference book for writers: *Jeff Herman's Guide to Book Publishers, Editors, and Literary Agents*

Approximate Lengths of Short Stories

    a. Flash Fiction – Up to 1000 words
    b. Short Short Story – Under 200 words
    c. Short Story – 2000 – 7500 words
    d. Novelette – (General Fiction) 7500 – 15,000 words
    e. Novelette – (SF & Fantasy) 7500 – 17,500 words
    f. Novella – (General Fiction) 15,000 – 30,000 words
    g. Novella – (SF & Fantasy) 17,500 – 40,000 words
    h. Novel – (General Fiction) Over 30,000 words
    i. Novel – (SF & Fantasy) Over 40,000 words

Short Story Writers

Try a sampling of some good short stories. These are a great way to get to know this fascinating way to write.

1. *The Selected Stories of Patricia Highsmith* – Patricia Highsmith
2. *Eighteen* – Jan Burke
3. *Learning to Kill* – Ed McBain
4. *Martian Chronicles, The Illustrated Man, Dandelion Wine* – Ray Bradbury
5. *Bradbury Stories – A Hundred of His Most Celebrated Stories* – Ray Bradbury
6. *Futures Mystery Anthology Magazine*
7. *Alfred Hitchcock Mystery Magazine*
8. *Ellery Queen Mystery Magazine*
9. *Raymond Chandler's Four Complete Novels* which includes *Farewell My Lovely* and *The Big Sleep*
10. Anything by Anna Katharine Green
11. Anything by Mary Roberts Rinehart
12. *From Light **TO DARK*** – G.B. Pool

A Sampling of Short Stories
by G.B. Pool

Just Like Old Times
From The Johnny Casino Casebook #1 -
Past Imperfect

Case #6: Just Like Old Times
Date: April 28, 2002
Location: Los Angeles, CA

Five days after renewing my P.I. license and working four days, two people died, one a friend, but I solved the case. Sad consolation. But even after spending nearly a week alone in a small motel in the desert, I still felt lousy.

I headed back to my place in the mountains outside L.A. early Sunday evening and got my usual table at Rusty's Diner. A local band was onstage. Somebody said they played backup in a recording studio down in Hollywood for a couple of Country Western singers, but I didn't recognize their names. Where I came from in New Jersey, "country" meant Canada and "western" meant Pennsylvania.

After ordering a beer and bratwurst, I sat back and listened to the music. It was starting to grow on me. At least you could understand the words. How bad could a guy be who loved his dog, his truck, and his girl?

My cell phone rang. I was lucky to get service that far back in the woods. Logjam was just about as far off the beaten track as you could get without ending up in Barstow.

"Hello?"

"Johnny, is that you?" I recognized Iris Sherwood's voice and shook my head.

Iris might have rented my other house down in Los Angeles, but I had spent quality time there over the past three years. The place was a bit of a relic, just like she was. Iris was Old Hollywood. Very Old Hollywood. She knew every actor who was anybody from the 30s through the 60s. Hedda Hopper would have hocked her hats for the scoops she could have gotten from the venerable star. But Iris, in her mid-eighties, knew how to keep secrets. And bless her heart, the old gal was a character herself, and that had nothing to do with the ones she played on the silver screen.

"You called me, Iris. What is it?"

"Oh, good, he's there," she said to someone with her on the other end of the phone. "Johnny, I need you."

"Is something wrong?" Two weeks earlier she really had a problem, so I couldn't say she always cried wolf.

"Nothing's wrong, silly. I want you to come for dinner tomorrow. Please say yes, Johnny, dear. It's time I did something nice for you."

"Dinner. Uh… I'm kinda tired, Iris."

"Tired! How can a young man like you be tired? I'm twice your age and never had a tired day in my life. Now, what do you say? Eight o'clock tomorrow. Okay?"

What the hell, I thought. Another change of scenery might be just what the doctor ordered. "Sure, Iris. Eight o'clock."

"We will be dressing for dinner, Johnny. Black tie," she added before hanging up.

I put down my cell phone and said out loud, "What did she expect me to do, come in my bathrobe?"

"Going someplace, Johnny?" said a voice to my right.

I turned to see Logjam's resident mortician. He wasn't the tall, gaunt, gray man from the Boris Karloff movies. Harold Kane was shorter, plumper, and pinker.

"I've been invited to dinner. The lady told me 'black tie.' Please tell me, in laid-back California terms, that doesn't mean tuxedo."

"Sorry, Johnny. I'd loan you one of ours, but they all button up the back. The Bridal Boutique next to Abigail's Flowers rents them."

"I thought I could get through my entire life without having to wear one of those get-ups. I wonder if I still have a tie."

"A bow tie," he clarified.

"Bow tie?"

"And opera slippers," he added.

"I'm not wearing slippers. I'll starve first."

"You're going to a formal dinner?" he questioned.

"Yeah. I guess. Can't I wear plain shoes to a fancy dinner?"

"They'll have to be patent leather."

"I'll be a customer of yours before I wear patent leather shoes, Harold."

"It's traditional."

"Are you telling me the guys wearing tuxedoes in the movies are wearing ballet shoes?"

"Opera slippers. And yes, probably."

"Oh, for crying out loud. James Bond? Bogart wore 'em?" He nodded. "No wonder they were tough guys. You'd have to be if you were wearing ballet slippers."

I spent my youth holed up in cheap hotel rooms watching old movies hour after hour on a 13-inch black and white TV set fitted with a pair of rabbit ears, waiting for sleazy little guys to bring me the take from the numbers operation I ran in Jersey for Big Louie "Fingers" D'Abruzzo, and then later when I busted heads down in Miami for Big Eddie "Mambo" Fontaine. And here I thought George Raft was tough. Ballet slippers. Ha!

The next day I bought myself a tuxedo and dress shoes. Not patent leather and not slippers, just plain black shoes. I had the clerk show me how to tie the frigging bow tie and how to strap on the cummerbund. All I kept thinking was, this better be a damn good dinner, Iris.

I'd been to other dinners at Iris's and met lots of Hollywood stars, but every time it was come-as-you-are. I usually wore slacks and a sports coat. Iris wore whatever odd get-up she concocted from her wardrobe confiscated from the studios. But never did I have to get dressed up in a tux. Oh well, there's a first time for everything.

The drive down the mountain into Los Angeles took two and a half hours. There wasn't much traffic coming from that direction, but it's still a long haul from my place on the lake to the Petit Palace north of Los Feliz Boulevard, as Iris called it. The six thousand square foot California villa was left to me in the will of a grateful client. All that gold trim and the painted ceilings and the Louis Something furniture was too much for an old boy from the rough side of Jersey City. The only painted ceilings I ever saw were done with a spray can.

If there is the reverse of claustrophobia, that house gave it to me. The joint had eight bathrooms and I'm pretty sure I never saw more than three of them. That's why I hired a real estate firm to rent it for me and I moved up here to yokeldom, where I rattle around in twenty-five hundred square feet of knotty pine. But with all the trees and ducks and bears and tourists, it still gives me that crowded, urban feeling.

As I pulled into the villa's circular drive in my SUV, I realized this wasn't the usual command performance. Iris hadn't mentioned who the other guests were, but from the cars in the drive, I figured they were from the higher echelon of relics from Hollywood's Golden Age. Three of the cars came with drivers decked out in black suits and cloth caps. They stood beside their vehicles polishing the antique paint. When I worked for Big Eddie in Miami, I'd take some of these beauties for collateral when my customers couldn't pay up. Sometimes Big Eddie would just take them… period.

The first car was a 1937 Cord Convertible, snow white, with its leather top down. Next to it was a black 1934 Ford Sedan. It looked like one of those cars Edward G. Robinson drove in his gangster movies. There was a pink Cadillac convertible, too. The 1959 Eldorado Biarritz had a set of fins that could swim to Catalina. And sitting all by itself under the arbor was a cherry-red Corvette, the 1958 model with white walls and chrome trim.

I love my SUV, but, oh, baby. My mouth was open and I was in serious jeopardy of stepping on my tongue.

"Careful, son. They're addictive."

Chalkie Parker was standing in the doorway smiling at me, looking dapper in a tuxedo, his silver hair shining in the porch light. He was Iris's manservant, her former lover, and her constant companion. Parker was also a world-class jewel thief who hung up his burglar tools before I was born. He was still wearing those white gloves and I think I figured out why. Fingerprints. His former occupation had him wanted on three continents.

"Don't tell me," I said. "Old fans are sending Iris tokens of their appreciation."

"And don't think she didn't get a few automobiles, my smart friend. But, alas, no. These belong to our…Iris's other guests." He noticed my duds. "You clean up good, Mr. Casino. A regular Cary Grant." He looked at my street shoes and smiled.

Just a few weeks earlier I had been sitting in the same house, having a quiet whiskey in the library with Parker. This night the villa had been transformed. It was the first time I really thought of the place as a palace. The crystal chandeliers sparkled brighter than a king's ransom. The walls glowed and it had nothing to do with the paint. The reason stood under the Italian chandelier in the foyer.

Iris.

Wearing a vintage lace gown with a high collar from one of her prehistoric movies, she was more radiant than the strands of pearls around her wizened neck. Her thinning hair was piled on her head like a queen's, and true to her style, she wore a tiara. Knowing Iris, those were real stones.

"Johnny! My hero!" She put her frail arm around my neck and pulled me close to her. Softly, she gave me a little kiss.

"Iris, I didn't do anything," I tried to say.

"Not the diamond caper," she whispered. "You're all over television. Private detective Johnny Casino saves congressman. I've told everybody that I know you personally, and we have been getting calls all week wanting to know when you'd be back in town and back in business."

"I'm not moving to Los Angeles, Iris. I'm gonna work out of Logjam."

"Logjam! Why? The action is here in L.A., big guy."

I heaved a sigh and hoped she'd go on to other things.

"Come and meet my other guests," she said. "They're dying to meet you. Oh, maybe at their ages, I shouldn't say 'dying.'" She winked and dragged me into the living room.

"My dears, may I present Johnny Casino, Private Eye."

I was instantly transported into the first reel of one of those film noirs I used to watch, except this one was in living color. I recognized the faces, even though they were several decades older in this version.

Jack Davis was the oldest actor there. He was doing tough-guy movies with Cagney when he was nineteen and love scenes with Crawford when he was twenty. His first acting job was in a crowd scene in a 1928 silent picture with Greta Garbo. He told Iris that Garbo talked more in the movie than she did on the set.

As for Jack, he loved to talk about every movie ever made. At 92, his memory was still as sharp as his attire. His suit looked like he had borrowed it from William Powell.

Vera Hollcroft was the kid in the group, only 84. She made a career playing the gorgeous gun moll in those 1940's flicks. You could see why the camera loved her back then. Her cheekbones still gave her face a glamorous look, even though her skin was wrinkled like old parchment. Her memory was failing, too, and half the time you'd think she was doing a scene from *Sunset Boulevard*, except Vera really thought DeMille would be calling her for that close-up.

Howard Anderson was the quiet one. He was blessed with a head of snow-white hair and was usually cast as the wise old family doctor. More than once he would slowly turn toward the other characters in the scene with him, shake that stately mane and solemnly pronounce, "I'm sorry. He's dead."

Rupert Campbell was wearing a charcoal gray pinstriped suit. He must have come in the Ford. He looked like a gangster. His hair had thinned to eight or ten strands that were now plastered over the top of his large head along with a handful of liver spots, but he still had a commanding look.

Rupe spent his entire career doing Mafioso types, yet when he read for the part Brando ended up getting in *The Godfather*, the producers said he didn't look Italian. His claim to fame was that he died in every movie he ever made. He'd recreate his death scene at the drop of a hat, even at the ripe old age of 90. He couldn't fall onto the carpet anymore, but he would slump into a chair and do the scene from a sitting position.

After the introductions, we ate. I didn't know people really lived like that. Imported caviar. French Champagne. Even the lobsters flew in from Maine. I wonder how they got through security.

For dessert Parker wheeled in a trolley with something fully engulfed in flame. I jumped out of my chair and was going to hit it with a pitcher of water before Iris calmed me down and told me it was supposed to be on fire. She called it Cherries Jubilee.

After five courses, we found ourselves sitting in the library enjoying after-dinner drinks. The liquor was good. Most of the geriatric crowd sipped theirs. As for me, I was trying hard to keep up with Rupert who could have drunk Richard Burton under the table. I had trained my palate to love 12-year old Scotch. I had no idea how good the 18-year old variety was. I do now. I was on my third shot when we settled in for what I figured would be an all-night gab session. Most of the movie stars the old fossils talked about during dinner had long since faded from the scene, but the stories were great.

"Clark was married to Joan at the time," said Vera. "I heard her tell the story to Natalie Moorhead."

"Gable was never married to Crawford," interrupted Howard. "But they did spend more time together making pictures than he did with his first wife. And you know Clark. He had gotten used to the good life by then. He was married to Rhea at that point. Joan was just another hoofer."

Iris shook her head. "No, no, no. Joan was out of the chorus line by 1928. She was a leading lady before Clark got his first speaking part."

"That's right," confirmed Jack. "It was 1931. Clark and Joan did three pictures that year. He did only one with Norma Shearer, *A Free Soul*."

"And from what I heard," said Vera, in what sounded like a stage whisper, "Adela Rogers St. Johns wrote that one especially for Joan, and Norma, that gorgeous cat, told Irving Thalberg she wanted it, or else."

"And whatever Norma wanted, Norma got," said Iris.

"She didn't get the Scarlett O'Hara part," said Jack.

"And you know why," said Iris, assuming everyone knew the story.

"She didn't like Clark Gable's wooden teeth," said Vera, getting her stories confused.

"Those were George Washington's wooden teeth," said Jack, correcting her.

That further befuddled Vera. "Clark Cable borrowed George Washington's teeth?"

Everyone took a healthy swallow of his or her drink. Everyone except Vera, who was still contemplating Clark Gable at Valley Forge.

I drank down the last of my Scotch and stood up to pour myself another drink. Parker might have been the butler during these soirees, but he was nodding off in a tall, wingback chair, not terribly interested in hearing stories he had listened to for fifty years. That's when I heard it. Parker's eyes twitched and he sat up. We were both looking at the library door when two armed men ran into the room.

"Hands up! All of you."

One man was in his late thirties, but he looked like he'd done hard time. Maybe it was the sallow complexion that said he'd spent three to five as a guest of the State. And his baggy clothes belonged to someone two sizes larger. The other guy was early-thirties, and his clothes fit better.

Parker stepped forward.

"Don't move, pops," said the older thug.

I glanced at Parker. He squeezed his elbow against his side like he was feeling for a shoulder holster and then looked at me. I shook my head slightly. He shrugged. I never go anywhere without packing heat except for that night, wearing that stupid monkey suit. I made a mental note to myself, to never, ever, leave home without a weapon again.

Not all of us in the room with the gunmen realized the gravity of the situation. Vera spoke first.

"Iris! Entertainment. How wonderful. This is a lot better than your last party, dear. But what does his costume represent?"

"She's right, Iris," said Howard. "He needs to borrow one of Jack's old pinstripes. Hey, Jack. You got one to fit this mug?"

"I'm not here for laughs, old man," said the guy. "Which one of you is Johnny Casino?"

All eyes turned in my direction. "I'm Johnny Casino. What can I do for you?"

"I need your help."

"Excuse me?"

He lowered his gun a fraction and I saw a plaintive look on his face. "You're supposed to be smart. I heard about you on TV."

"This isn't exactly the place to talk business," I said. "Let's leave here and—"

"No!" barked the other guy, waving his revolver. "We stay here. These old folks are our hostages."

"Hostages?" questioned Vera. "What does he mean hostages? Have we been kidnapped?"

"It's okay, Vera," said Jack. "This punk won't be here long."

"Whadda ya mean, punk?" said the punk with the itchy trigger-finger. "I've been in jail."

"And you'll be doing a return engagement quite shortly," said Jack.

"Why you old—"

"Shut up, Beans," said the brains of the outfit.

"If you want me," I said, "you'll have to let these folks go."

"That's not the way it's going down, Casino," said the leader. He wiped the sweat off his forehead before adding, "They're my leverage. Get rid of the kitchen help. No funny business or somebody will get hurt. Beans, you go with him."

"Sure, Mike. Come on, Casino."

With Beans standing just outside the kitchen door, jabbing me in the back with his gun, I managed to dismiss the caterer and her staff with a hurried explanation and a handful of bills.

Returning to the library, I was faced with wide eyes and worried looks.

"What do you want?" I asked this Mike character.

"Beans, you watch these old people while I take Casino here for a little ride. And Beans, do... not... hurt... them... in... any... way."

He gave his instructions like he was writing them on a chalkboard in large block letters. Beans let the words sink in like a dog learning a new trick.

"Okay, okay, boss. You be back soon?"

"When I'm through with Casino."

"Don't you dare hurt him," said Iris, standing up to the hoodlum.

"Don't worry, lady," said Mike. "He's only in trouble if he doesn't help me."

Mike motioned me to leave. I gave a slight shrug to Parker and headed through the foyer and out the front door. We walked past the chauffeurs, down the driveway, and finally to a beat-up Chevy parked two blocks away.

"Just tell me what this is all about," I pleaded. "I don't want Beans to do anything to those old folks."

"He won't hurt 'em. His gun isn't even loaded." I started to move toward him. "Mine, on the other hand, is. But I'll tell you this, Mr. Casino, I have no intention of hurting you. I need your help."

"You have a strange way of asking for it. What kind of trouble are you in?"

"I want you to solve a murder."

"Is that why you were in jail?"

"I see you recognized my jailhouse tan? But, I was in for robbery, not murder."

"Who do they think you killed?"

"I don't know," he said.

"I don't get it. Why do you think they'll blame you?"

"Get in the car and I'll tell you."

I opened the passenger door and started to get in. I could see another man in the seat.

"Excuse me," I said. The man didn't answer. "Uh, do you want me to get in the back?" Silence. I stood up and asked Mike, "What am I supposed to do here?"

"Find out who this guy is..." With a slight touch of Mike's hand, the stiff fell forward. "And who killed him."

"If it were me, I'd push him off a cliff and let somebody else find him. Why don't you just go to the police?"

"With my record? I'm not supposed to associate with felons. Just think what the cops would do if I turned up with this guy."

"You associate with Beans."

"I don't know anybody else dumb enough to pull a stunt like this, Mr. Casino."

"Call me Johnny."

"My name is Mike Levine. I am...or was, a bank robber by trade."

"Your friend, Beans, is in that house scaring the hell out of those people. Let's do our talking back there."

"You'll help me?"

"You have any money?"

"Where's the nearest bank?"

We both grinned.

We went back to the house. The scene had changed slightly since our departure. The seniors were sitting at a table playing cards. Beans was tied up on the floor.

"That didn't take long," said Parker.

"I was going to say the same thing. How did you...?" I indicated the trussed up punk.

"Iris hit him over the head with a silver tray and I hit him with a Louis 15th chair. I hated to do it. It was a lovely chair. Johnny, his gun wasn't even loaded. What's this all about?"

"I think Mr. Levine is about to tell us," I said to Parker. "Pour us another drink and we'll straighten this out."

Somebody suggested we untie Beans. He's lucky we didn't take a vote because he would have lost. Soon afterward we got down to business.

"Who has it in for you?" I asked Mike.

He didn't hesitate. "Vincent Merrick. I used to work for him."

"What does he do?" I asked.

"Owns a bank."

"Did you rob it?"

"This man's a kidnapper *and* a bank robber!" exclaimed Vera.

"We're not kidnapped anymore, dear," said Iris.

"I robbed banks when Merrick needed a cash infusion," said Mike. "I never hit his place."

"Why would he dump the dead guy on you?"

"What dead guy?" asked Rupert.

"Is this the plot to a new movie?" asked Vera.

"Hush," said Iris.

"As soon as I got out of jail he wanted me back working for him," explained Mike. "Look, Johnny, I've got a girl now. I want to go straight. He won't let me."

"Does he have anything on you…except the stiff in the car?"

"Yeah. I finger him and he tells the cops about all the other jobs I pulled. I'll do twenty years."

"You must have been pretty good," I said.

"He couldn't be that good," said Rupert. "He got caught."

"I let myself get caught," said Mike. "I wanted out."

"Why would a banker have you rob other banks?" I asked.

"He needed money. He lives large, and frankly, he has a mean streak."

"How many banks did you have to knock over to keep him happy?" asked Howard.

"None were big takes. Four, five hundred thousand a job. I'd do three, four heists a year."

"Were the other bankers in on it?" I asked.

"No. But he knew who would be making large deposits."

"That was convenient," said Howard.

"Nothing convenient about it," said Mike.

"That reminds me of a picture Rupe and I did back in '42," said Jack. "*Death Comes Knocking*. Rupe's character was knee-deep in debt. He forces me to rob him so he can collect the insurance money."

"Yeah. But I get mine in the end," said Rupert. "I had a great death scene in that picture. Five lines." He paused to recall his exact dialogue. Getting into character, he said, "Is diss how you pay me back? Wid a bullet. I pulled you outta da gutter. You were nothin' without Big Frankie. You'll be nothin' again. Nothin', ya see. I made you." He coughed twice.

Rupert dropped his head onto the card table and theatrically expired. We all watched in rapt amazement. Mike looked at Rupert, and then looked at me.

"I think Vince Merrick blackmails his accomplices, too."

"Blackmail!" said Iris. "The swine."

"How does he get them to go along with him?" I asked.

"He must have somebody on the inside telling him who's vulnerable," Mike said.

"You did three, four robberies a year?" I asked. He nodded. "It would be hard to plant someone inside each business with that much success. What did these suckers have in common?"

"Most of them had businesses in the Bonaventure Hotel," said Mike. "That's where Merrick's bank is."

"That sounds more like a bug infestation," I said.

"What are you talking about, Johnny?" asked Jack. "A cockroach with a tape recorder?"

"Not quite, Mr. Davis," I said. "You can bug an office with something no bigger than a breath mint nowadays."

"Can I say something?" asked Beans, who had been sitting quietly on the sofa.

"Make it short," said Mike.

"Why don't we dump the stiff back in Mr. Merrick's lap? I never liked him anyway."

The group looked at each other and then at Beans. We had to admit, the idiot had a good idea.

"Hmm," I said, pondering the punk's suggestion. "Maybe we can kill two birds with one stone. Mike, has Merrick told you who the next victim is?"

"Yeah. We were gonna use a guy we hit the year before I got busted, but Merrick changed his mind. Now it's an import/export guy."

"Why did he change victims?" I asked.

"I really don't know. It's the first time one of his marks backed out. But I'm not in on the set up. Merrick does all the arm twisting himself."

"What was the other guy's name?" I asked.

"Armand Boussac."

Iris gasped.

"You know him?" I asked her.

"I buy some of my jewelry from Armand. He serves such wonderful teacakes in his delightful little shop."

I had a thought. "Iris, what does Armand look like?"

"Fernando Lamas. Only shorter."

I looked over at Mike. "That pretty well describes the stiff in your car, doesn't it, Mike?"

"Sure does."

"That explains Merrick's change of plans," said Rupert. "Okay, Johnny, what do we do next?"

I looked at Rupert and then noticed all the old fools were smiling at me. "I work alone, folks." They kept smiling. "Really. This could get dangerous."

"This reminds me of a picture I saw in '65," said Jack. "*The Game Never Ends*. It was one of those new-fangled anti-hero plots where everybody was a thief, but the movie had this clever twist..."

Jack explained the film. I could tell before he got to the final credits he had outlined a winning plan. My only hope was that Vincent Merrick never saw the movie.

It took twenty-four hours to plot our strategy.

The first thing Wednesday morning Iris & entourage arrived at the front desk of the Bonaventure. Parker had called ahead for reservations and asked the hotel manager to arrange assistance for two invalid women who would be arriving in wheelchairs, one being famed screen actress, Iris Sherwood. The group, including "Doctor" Howard Anderson, was escorted to two of the glass elevators and then to a suite of rooms on one of the upper floors. It was an expensive suite, so the help was lavish.

At about the same time, Jack Davis's driver drove up to the entrance in the '37 Cord and helped the old man out of the car and into a small, collapsible wheelchair that he pulled from the trunk. Jack wheeled himself into the lobby and made his way to The Bistro, where he sat and ordered coffee and crullers. He had positioned his chair as close to the entrance to Merrick's bank as he could before he placed what looked like a radio on the table and adjusted a generic walkman headset over his ears. He sat there tapping his fingers to imaginary music.

Mike went to Merrick's bank before they opened for business, and said he would go along with the heist, but he said he wanted a bigger cut. One greedy guy understands another. The deal was set. As Mike left Merrick's office, he placed a small listening device under the desk. I had done a little shopping the day before and secured a few electronic toys. I was surprised how sophisticated the gadgets had become while I was retired.

Now it was my turn. I parked a rented van with a hydraulic lift tailgate in an outside lot and walked to the hotel. I wasn't alone. In a wheelchair scrubbed of any fingerprints was poor Mr. Boussac, covered with a blanket around his shoulders and over his lap and a hat pulled low over his face.

I was dressed like an orderly, with white cotton gloves. I continually bent over my charge taking silent orders from a very demanding corpse.

"Yes, Mr. Jones. I'll get you a nice cup of tea. What?… Of course. Would you like your usual table?… Yes, sir. Right away."

We picked an ordinary name for our unwanted guest and hoped for the best. The plan was that no one would recognize Boussac if we had him bundled up like a beggar.

On cue I rolled him up to Jack's table.

"Why, Fred. You old scoundrel," Jack said to the dead guy.

I reached under the blanket and managed to lift Boussac's arm just enough so Jack could grab the hand and shake it. At just that moment the waitress sidled up.

"Hello, Monsieur Boussac. Your usual?" she said, giving him her best bucktoothed grin.

Oh, Christ, I thought. I shoulda wrapped Boussac up in bandages before dragging him out in public. One yelp out of the waitress when she sizes up the stiff, and the entire Over-The-Hill gang will be sharing digs at San Quentin. Fortunately, my Thespian friend knew what to do when an actor forgets his lines.

Jack turned his back to the woman and in a low tone ad-libbed a very raspy, "Oui,"

I leaned over the dead man and began patting him on the back, emitting small coughs as I did. "You stay wrapped up, sir. Cough, cough. No need spreading that flu bug to everybody."

The waitress backed away as Jack continued, "Bring me another cup of coffee, my dear. And my friend's usual."

"Yes, sir." She scooted off.

"Now what?" asked Jack, panicked that Boussac's cover was blown.

"We play it by ear. Speaking of ear, have you overheard anything?"

"Merrick's a full-fledged pig. He called the import/export guy on his speakerphone the minute Mike left and told him to get down to his office on the double."

At that moment, the glass elevator behind us descended. A short Chinese man made a beeline to Merrick's bank.

"That must be him," said Jack. "He sounded like Charlie Chan."

The bank still wasn't open, but a small staff was getting ready for the business day to begin. A tall woman in a skin-tight suit that said she was more into pleasure than business unlocked the door and let the nervous man enter. His eyes dropped to the ground when he saw her. She jerked her head in the direction of Merrick's office. He slunk into the room. I grabbed the earphones and listened.

"I cannot do this, Mr. Merrick," said a heavily accented voice. "It not good."

"I can ruin you with one phone call, Mr. Chang. Anyway, what have you got to lose? Your bank's insured."

"But—"

"Did you tell your buyer you had to be paid in cash?"

"Yes. I tell him my offshore investment company trade only in cash. He understand."

"I just bet he did. You two be at Taipei Bank at exactly ten o'clock tomorrow. It shouldn't take more than thirty minutes to make the transfer and get that money in the bank manager's hot little hands. The minute we see you step out of his office with the receipt, we'll make our move."

"What you promise me. When do I get it?" asked Chang.

"It'll be delivered to your shop by courier after you visit your bank."

"But no more, Mr. Merrick," said Chang. "No more."

If that was a threat, it was a lousy one. Mr. Chang left Merrick's office, his head still down as he shuffled out of the bank. I heard Merrick's secretary walk into his office, but I wanted to follow Chang instead of listening. I handed the earphones back to Jack and sprinted after the man. We rode the elevator to the fifth floor and got out.

I didn't know what to make of this guy. It sounded like he was in on the heist after all and I wanted to get the goods on him. He slowly unlocked his shop's door and went in, locking it behind him. Watching him through the large, plate-glass window, he slowly sat himself behind a hand-carved teakwood desk and bowed his head. Finally he dropped his head into his hands and cried.

"Hmm," I said to myself.

I got on one of the three glass elevators in that sector. Another elevator stopped on the same floor within eyeshot. I watched as a man jerked his head to tell his woman to get on board. When she didn't move fast enough, he grabbed her arm and shoved her inside. Her eyes dropped to the floor in submission as they rode out of sight. It was the same submissive expression Chang had on his face when Merrick's secretary was brow beating him earlier.

I opened my cell phone and called Parker. "I know how Merrick gets his victims." I explained my theory and told him what to do.

The first thing I noticed when I got to the lobby was that our dear, departed friend had departed.

"Where's Boussac?" I asked.

"Rupert thought he should get him out of the way since the waitress recognized him. He took him up to the suite."

"We need him down here before Iris makes her move."

"I'll ring his room," said Jack.

"Anything going on in the bank?" I asked.

"Lots of heavy breathing in Merrick's office."

"The secretary's still in there?"

"Some secretary."

"Yeah. I think the lady is our common denominator."

At just that moment, the woman came out of Merrick's office. She headed for the teller windows while fastening the top button of her blouse and fixing her lipstick. That's when Merrick's phone rang.

"This should be it," I said. "Tell Rupert to return Boussac."

Merrick wasn't using the speakerphone this time, but I didn't need to hear the other side of the conversation. I knew what the dapper man on the other end was asking. His employer had a small fortune in jewels that needed safekeeping for two or three days while she was staying in town. She refused to let the hotel take charge of them because she had seen too many movies about famous women having their jewels stolen in these fancy hotels.

Merrick asked the name of this grande dame. He actually knew Iris Sherwood's name and reputation. Iris will be happy to know she wasn't forgotten.

"I'll be more than glad to keep Miss Sherwood's jewels in my safe. Can you give me an estimate of their value? I'll probably have to add extra security. No additional cost to you, of course."

I could just imagine Merrick's reaction when Parker rattled off the seven-figure sum in his greedy little ear.

"I'll make all the arrangements, Mr. Parker. I'll call you back in one hour so we can make sure the transfer is secure."

No sooner did he hang up than he dialed another number. I knew his next call would be to Mike Levine.

I turned to update Jack, but he was still on his cell phone. I mouthed the name: Rupert? He shook his head. He mouthed: Iris. I shrugged and mouthed: What? He handed me the phone.

"What is it, Iris?"

"It's Vera. You better come."

I rode the space age elevator through the glass ceiling in the hotel's atrium and found myself clinging to the side of that ultramodern edifice. The elevator pod was now on the exterior of the building. On the 28th floor, Howard was at their door hurrying me along.

"What is it?" I asked.

"Stage fright," said Howard, his white hair looking a little frazzled.

"Pay attention, Vera," Iris was saying. "It's very simple. You want to close your account. You wheel yourself up to the teller and say your lines."

Vera was getting flustered. She tried to get into character. "But, Iris, I don't have an account at that bank." Her tiny eyes looked lost behind those high cheekbones.

"I know, dear, but they don't. Now you have to get this right. Try it again."

Vera wheeled her chair around and faced Iris who was standing behind the bar in the hotel room. She took a deep breath and said, "I'm here to rob the bank."

"No, Vera," said Iris. "You don't want to rob it. You want to close your account. Try again."

"How long has this been going on?" I asked Howard.

"Since we got here. She has that line in her head and we can't shake it loose."

"Vera," I said, turning her around and looking into those scared eyes. "This is a major role. You must believe that you have money in that bank. You feel it here." I patted my chest. "Now we'll go downstairs and you make them believe it. Are you ready?" I framed her face like framing a camera angle and slowly backed away. "Action."

Parker pushed Iris. Howard had Vera. And I took Mr. Boussac. We rode separate elevators. I looked at my watch. Right on time.

Iris and Parker were the first customers of the day. Merrick was on them like a rash.

"You're early," he said. "I haven't finished making the arrangements." He couldn't keep his eyes off the two large jewelry boxes on Iris's lap. "Wait in my office." He ushered them partway through the security door, the exact time Vera and "Doctor" Anderson made their entrance. Vera's voice echoed through the ultra modern bank.

"Service! Service, please," she said.

Merrick snapped his fingers and one of the tellers waved her over. Howard hobbled across the floor, giving me time to push Boussac near the deposit slip counter in the center of the room. I pulled out a form and started writing on it, holding my breath until Vera spoke. Meanwhile Parker managed to stick a small magnetic device across the electronic latch going to the office and vault areas.

Vera eased herself to the edge of her wheelchair and looked the teller in the eye. I saw her chest rise as she inhaled deeply and then said in a very clear voice. "I'm here to… close my account."

Breathing again, I watched as Vera continued her scene. In less than forty-five seconds it was discovered that she had no account at the bank.

"Thieves!" yelled Vera. "Thieves!" she yelled again.

Iris and Parker were just getting settled in Merrick's office. Vera's outburst brought him running. While Merrick was putting out that fire, Jack rolled into the bank in his wheelchair and positioned himself directly behind me. If I got the placement right, the surveillance cameras would see him enter, but they couldn't see him sitting behind me from any angle.

I looked at the clock. Zero hour.

Mike stormed in wearing a ski mask and waving a gun. "This is a holdup!" He pushed the front doors shut and flipped the CLOSED sign into view. "Everybody into the back. Move it!"

A teller released the catch on the security door so we could enter the rear. Wheelchairs were rolled into the safe deposit area. It was Vera and Howard, Boussac and me, two tellers, the sexy secretary, Merrick, and Mike. Funny, only the tellers looked nervous, really nervous. As for Jack, he was kneeling behind the center counter. I had hooked his folded wheelchair on the back of Boussac's chair under the blanket.

Mike pointed to Merrick. "You. In the vault."

Merrick led the way. In the hallway I could just barely hear him whisper to Mike, "You're half an hour early. I haven't got the jewels yet."

Mike tapped his watch. "It's broken."

"Steal a new one," growled Merrick.

Before Mike could push Merrick into the office, Iris wheeled herself into the hallway. Mike spotted the jewel cases.

"My lucky day. I'll take those, lady."

Mike grabbed the boxes and was turning to leave when he ran smack dab into Rupert who had used the electronic release I provided to unlatch the security door after entering the bank.

"Excuse me," said Rupert. "The doors were closed during business hours. Hey, what's…"

"Out of my way, old man," said Mike.

"Why you young—"

A shot rang out. Rupe grabbed his chest and then slumped on the counter. "I knew there was trouble," he said. "I only wanted to help." He coughed twice before sinking slowly to the floor.

Mike dropped the jewel cases and fled. "Doctor" Anderson stepped out of the safe deposit room and spotted the man on the floor. He knelt beside him and felt for a pulse. Then, looking up, he said solemnly, "I'm sorry. He's dead."

Iris yelled, "My jewels! My jewels!"

I was standing behind Howard. I retrieved the cases and handed them to Iris. "What's this?" I picked up a small tape recorder. "The robber must have dropped it."

I ran it back until it stopped and then hit the play button. We all heard Merrick's voice loud and clear, "They're in there. Take the two jewel cases and leave."

"It looks like you're in deep trouble, Mr. Merrick," said Howard. "Someone call the police."

"I'll do it," said the secretary.

"I'll go with you," I said, "You, too, Merrick."

I followed them to the front. She started dialing a long number. I took the phone out of her hand and dialed a shorter one: 9-1-1.

Now it was Iris's turn. She raced her wheelchair from the hallway into the main room. "I want to go home. I knew I'd get robbed if I went out. Home, Parker."

Parker came up behind her and pushed the wheelchair across the room. Vera got her chariot into high gear with Howard chugging to keep up.

"Watch Merrick," I said to Parker.

I went back for Boussac and wheeled him into Merrick's office. I pulled the blanket from around his shoulders and retrieved the one on his lap as well as the hat. I opened the smaller wheelchair and popped it into position.

I could see Parker had done his job while in the office alone. Mike thought Merrick was blackmailing his victims. The leggy distraction in the tight suit looked like my idea of a high-priced leisure activity. I told Parker to search for photographic evidence used in blackmail. The wall safe was open and a stack of videotapes was on the desk. Motion pictures would cost a target even more than a photograph. I grabbed the one with Boussac's name on it and tucked it next to him. I stuffed another one into the pocket of my white coat before pushing the smaller wheelchair into the main bank area, having picked up a passenger along the way. Rupert, back from the dead, wrapped the blankets around himself as I pushed him into view.

It was a three-ring circus in there. Wheelchairs were rolling as the sound of sirens filled the air.

The cops cuffed Merrick on Iris's say-so. Who's to argue with a legend? The secretary wouldn't get far, once the District Attorney ran the videotape of her seducing the late Mr. Boussac.

A while later, I rode the elevator one more time. I'd done it so often I was getting the bends.

I went to Mr. Chang's shop. It was still locked. I knocked and waved the videocassette at him. With a questioning look on his face, he slowly approached and then unlocked the door.

"I believe this is yours," I said.

Jack was waiting for me when I got on the elevator to go back down. He said, "Johnny, this isn't the way that movie ended. The s.o.b. did it alone."

I looked out the glass capsule at my splendid cast of characters waiting below. "Life isn't a movie."

"JUST LIKE OLD TIMES" ORIGINALLY PUBLISHED BY
TOP PUBLICATIONS IN *LANDMARKED FOR MURDER* IN 2006.

IN THE NICK OF TIME

"Is he dead?"

"If he isn't, the cold will finish him off. Go through his pockets."

"Why do I have to do it?"

"You're the junior partner," said Vinnie while he tugged the ski jacket around his ample belly. He tried it on at a local ski shop and then walked out the door with it. The security tag was still attached, but he cut it off, taking a walnut size piece of cloth and padding with it.

"Since when did I get to be the *junior* partner?" said Larry. He was a foot shorter than his buddy, and stringy like an old chicken. "I'm the one who told you this place was a goldmine." He leaned down and tentatively rummaged through the man's pockets. He didn't want to get too friendly, but he could hear the jingle of loose change. He jammed his hand into the front pocket and came back with a fist full of coins.

"Get his wallet," said Vinnie, reaching out and taking the money.

"I'll have to roll him over," said Larry, straightening and giving an involuntary shiver. An icy gust stung his eyes, the only exposed part under his ski mask.

"He won't care. Just do it."

"When do I get to be an equal partner?" mumbled Larry. "This was my idea."

"You saw an ad on the bus about skiing with the rich and famous and thought we might score big-time up here. I'm the one who thought about hitchhiking to this godforsaken place. I paid for the hotel room. And you don't even know how to ski."

"And I suppose you do?"

"Just roll him over."

"I need help," said Larry, still not wanting to kneel down near the body.

"Get your hands under him and lift. Gravity will do the rest."

Larry sighed. He got down in the snow along the path and thought about it. "He looks heavy."

"Oh, for crying out loud."

Vinnie dropped heavily to his knees and got both his arms underneath the man's designer ski parka and lifted. Obviously the man laying in the snow wasn't all that heavy, because he flipped over easily and rolled down the steep embankment. He had enough momentum to start a small avalanche, gathering snow as he rolled along.

Twenty feet below the ridge the snowman came to an abrupt stop against a small stand of trees. The snowball exploded in a shower of flakes as both men looked on.

"Yep," said Larry. "Gravity works."

"Oh, shut up. Let's get down there and finish the job."

"At least he's off the road," said Larry. "Somebody could have seen us." He yanked off his ski mask and stuffed it in his pocket. His shaggy brown hair stood up like a punk rocker's.

"It's lunchtime. All those snobs at the lodge are chowing down in the dining room."

"I could use something to eat myself," said Larry, hearing his stomach growl under the secondhand jacket he wore. It was one of Vinnie's hand-me-downs. Larry was swimming in it. "I think I'll take his scarf. I'm freezing."

"And somebody sees you wearing it and recognizes it. No way. You can buy yourself a new one with the loot we'll make."

Larry sighed again. "How are we gonna get down there?"

Vinnie checked out the road. There was no easy way to access the narrow valley below them from the ridge road. "You go down. Slide on your butt if you have too."

"Me?"

"This was your brilliant idea. Get going."

Larry harrumphed. "Next time I'm on a bus, I hope I see a picture of the beach."

He stumbled down the side of the hill, going knee deep in snow that had been shot over the edge by a county snow blower. He finally got to the body and stood there with his hands on his skinny hips.

"Now what?" yelled Vinnie.

"He landed on his back." Larry stared at the neatly cropped salt and pepper beard on the man's face. It was now full of snow, and icicles were forming along the jaw line.

"Roll him over."

Larry tugged at the guy's jacket and managed to get the body to cooperate. He reached for the man's back pocket when he heard Vinnie yelling. "Duck. Duck."

Larry looked up into the sky but didn't see anything.

"Somebody's coming, you idiot," shouted Vinnie. "Get out of sight."

Larry dived into the snow beside the guy in the red parka. He burrowed down as far as he could go and covered his head. Only his rear end was sticking up.

Vinnie started walking casually along the road like he had a reason to be there as the ski patrol vehicle drove up along side him and stopped.

"You okay, fella?" asked the ranger, rolling down the window. He looked like Dudley Do-Right, right down to the cleft in his chin and the full head of blond hair.

"Yeah. Just getting some exercise, if it's alright with you." Vinnie knew that last part sounded snarky, but he couldn't help himself.

"You got a car someplace?"

"I walked out here. I'll walk back."

The ranger noticed Vinnie's nice jacket. "You staying at the lodge?"

Vinnie put his elbow over the hole in the side of the coat. "Yeah. Great place."

"Okay. Merry Christmas, buddy."

"Dudley" rolled up his window and headed down the road. Vinnie waited until the vehicle was out of sight and then rushed back to the spot where Larry had climbed over. He gave his pal the all clear. When Larry finally struggled up the hill to the road, Vinnie put out his hand and Larry reached for it.

"No. The wallet. Gimme the wallet." Larry handed it over. "Three hundred and sixty bucks," Vinnie said after he opened all the little flaps. "Three hundred and sixty lousy bucks. That's all he had on him?" He looked at Larry with questioning eyes.

"I didn't take anything," He opened his jacket and dared his partner to search him. "Let's go back to the hotel. I'm cold and hungry."

They walked to the lodge. It was a long, frosty walk. Vinnie wouldn't speak to his pal. He gave Larry dirty looks the entire way. Larry squinted right back at him.

The men shared a small room at the rear of the four-story hotel. It was the cheapest accommodation in the place. Vinnie made himself a cup of coffee with the in-room coffee maker while Larry took a hot shower and changed into drier pants. Then they headed for the dining room and something to eat.

The place was abuzz. The holiday crowd was usually boisterous, but this time they were uncommonly disturbed. A cluster of après-ski clad folks bunched around a large blond woman who had become very animated.

"My husband's out there in the snow and a blizzard's coming. What am I going to do?"

"Did he go with anyone, Mrs. Whitman?" asked a guy in a deep blue ski sweater.

"No. He went by himself along the upper road. He wanted to take a walk before lunch."

"What was he wearing?" asked a lady in a dove grey ski outfit.

"A red parka and a yellow and white scarf. His school colors."

Vinnie elbowed Larry. "See. I told you so."

"Gosh. I hope he was bundled up well enough to handle the weather," said another man. "That storm looks like a bad one." He shook his head.

"But he wasn't wearing gloves or a hat," said the worried wife. "Just that six-carat diamond on his hand. That won't keep him warm. Oh, what will I do? What will I do?"

"The rangers are out looking for him right now, Mrs. Whitman. Don't worry. They'll find him." The man in the blue sweater put his arm around the woman as the other people tried to console her.

Mrs. Whitman, her eyes wide with fear, looked up. "What will I tell the children? It's Christmas Eve. They'll want their father." She collapsed against the man next to her.

Larry had been watching the scene, biting his lower lip. "Gee. That's tough."

Vinnie pulled him off to the side. "We have to go back."

"You're right. They need to know what happened to him."

"Not for the guy. For the diamond. Come on."

"I don't know," Larry said, holding back. "Look. Maybe we should just go get something to eat."

"Think about what we can buy after we sell that rock," said Vinnie, rubbing his hands together.

The pair headed out again on foot. The lodge provided snow boots, so they tramped along the road away from the warmth of the ski lodge and made their way to the location overlooking the valley below.

"What if we don't get back before the storm hits?" asked Larry.

"We've got plenty of time."

Larry looked up. The blue sky was turning purple and the breeze had picked up.

They found the spot where they had accidentally rolled the guy over the precipice.

"I don't see him," said Larry, straining to see into the pile of snow near the trees below.

"He's got to be there," said Vinnie, his voice anxious. "He's got to."

Vinnie charged over the edge. His weight had him sinking into the drifts up to his thighs. It was slow going, but finally they both got to the broken snowball that had entombed the man in the red parka.

"He's gone, Vinnie." Larry dropped down and began digging in the snow.

Vinnie looked around the area. "Somebody found him. Look." He pointed to large boot tracks leading away from them. The tread didn't fit either of their snow boots. "Somebody carried him off."

"They didn't take him back to the lodge, or we would have seen them," said Larry.

"A sleigh," said Vinnie. "Here are the tracks leading that way." He pointed into the woods.

"A sleigh? You mean like Santa Claus?" Larry looked heavenward.

"Yeah, Doofus. Santa came down and picked him up. And he'll get the diamond, if we don't find them first. Come on."

They followed the tracks of a one horse sleigh as it disappeared into the forest. It wasn't long before they came across a tiny cabin. A thin wisp of smoke was coming out of the chimney. Vinnie and Larry slowly approached the small house and peered in the grimy front window.

A man in a red parka huddled near a small fire burning in the fireplace. His back was to the window. There wasn't anyone else in the cabin.

"He must have gotten rid of the body and stole the jacket," whispered Vinnie.

"Did he take the ring?" asked Larry.

"I can't tell. Come on," he said, marching toward the door. "It's two against one."

Vinnie pushed open the door. The man by the fireplace jumped to his feet and turned around.

"It's you," said Larry, recognizing the man from the snowdrift.

"Thank God, you found me," said the man. "I thought I'd be out here 'til the spring thaw. But I didn't hear your car."

"We walked," said Larry.

"You walked? How far away from the lodge are we?"

"Not far," said Vinnie, looking around the room. A wooden table and two chairs sat under the window. A well-worn couch rested in front of the fireplace. Some cabinets, open and bare, were against another wall. He noticed an old set of fireplace tools on the wide hearth.

"What happened?" Larry asked.

"I had a seizure on the upper road. I passed out and must have rolled down the hill. I came to under a big tree and heard bells. One of the sleigh horses from the lodge must have gotten loose and was breathing in my face. I hoped the horse would get me back to the hotel, but we ended up here. I unhitched him and put him in the shed out back, came in the cabin, and built the fire."

"Why don't you warm up a little more before we head back," said Vinnie, inching his way toward the hearth.

"Great idea. I like cold weather, but this was a little much, even for me." He sat on the couch and gazed into the fire.

Larry plopped down next to the man. The firelight enhanced the deep wrinkles on the guy's forehead and the crinkles around his eyes. "How do you feel?" he asked, leaning closer to get a better view of the older man.

"I feel fine now." He turned and looked at Larry. "I can't believe you two walked out in the snow to find me. Not many strangers would put themselves out like that."

"We found your wallet in the snow," blurted Larry. "Didn't we, Vinnie?"

Vinnie had his hand nearly around the fireplace poker. He jerked up straight. "Yeah. Here it is." He dug into his jacket pocket. "I had to go through everything to see who owned it. You didn't have any credit cards."

"Never use them," said the man, leaning forward, taking the wallet. He stuffed it in his pants pocket without going through the cash. "Thanks so much. You two really are extraordinary. It does my heart good to see two guys who are down on their luck being so honest."

Vinnie tried covering up the hole in his ill-fitting parka while Larry tugged at the faulty zipper of his own jacket.

"You could have done a lot with that money. I owe you."

"We don't want anything," said Larry. "We're just glad you're okay."

"We should go now," said Vinnie.

The older man stood. He was a bit rocky on his feet. Larry slid an arm around his back and helped steady him.

"Thank you, son. What time is it?" He looked at his watch. It was an expensive gold one. Vinnie and Larry caught a glimpse of the big diamond ring on his finger, too. It was so heavy, it rolled to one side.

"Getting on to dinnertime. I hope they have something hearty tonight at the lodge. I could eat a bear." He gave a deep laugh that rumbled through the cabin.

They stepped outside. A cold wind whipped through the trees and bit their faces. Dark clouds were rolling in like a tidal wave.

"Go hitch up the sleigh, Larry," said Vinnie.

"Why don't you come with me, Vinnie?" Larry's eyes jumped between his partner and the older man with the grizzled beard who was leaning against the porch railing.

"You do it. We'll stay here," said Vinnie.

Larry's eyes dropped to Vinnie's empty hands.

"Okay. Don't... go anywhere."

Larry hitched up and then led the horse drawn sleigh to the front of the small log cabin.

"Let me put out the fire," said Vinnie. "I'll be back in a minute." He went into the cabin and partially shut the door.

As Larry was going to help the man into the sled, he asked, "What's your name?"

"Nicholas. You can call me Nick."

"Nick? Like St. Nick? And look, it's Christmas Eve. Gee." Larry lowered his head and fiddled with the reins for a second. "I'm glad you're not... I'm glad you are all right. How many kids you got?"

Nick wasn't listening. He had turned his head and was looking at the door behind him. "Give me a second."

He pushed inside the cabin.

"Vinnie? That's your name, isn't it?" he said to Vinnie's back. The heavyset guy with the greasy black hair turned around. "I want to thank you for all you've done." He reached into his pocket and pulled out the wallet. "Here. Take this." He handed Vinnie all the bills. "It's not much, but... I don't know. Maybe it's the season, but thanks. Split it with your buddy." He stared at the man standing by the fireplace. Vinnie looked away and shuffled his feet. "Lesser men would have kept the money. I've learned something from you."

He folded Vinnie's hand over the bills, turned, and walked out on the porch. He was in the sleigh beside Larry when Vinnie stepped outside.

Vinnie climbed aboard, took the reins, and they went back to the lodge.

Everyone else must have been out in the snow looking for the lost man, because there were no people clustered around the front door.

"Let me off at the side door, fellas," said Nick. "I want to go to my room first." He got out and went in the service entrance while Vinnie and

Larry took the sleigh around to the rear and left it with a young stable boy near the barn.

Then the pair went inside the lodge.

They were wrong about everyone being out searching for the missing man. The huge open room with the biggest fireplace was full of people, all talking at once, happy and excited. Mrs. Whitman walked amongst the crowd, shaking their hands, tears in her eyes, but she was overjoyed.

She finally got over to where the pair was standing. "Thank you. Thank you. He's fine. I appreciate all your help. Everyone has been so nice."

"I'm glad Nick is okay," said Larry.

"Nick? My husband's name is John. You do know the ranger found him at the wayfarer's chapel down the road. He had been mugged, robbed."

"Robbed?" questioned Vinnie.

"Yes. The thief stole his parka and scarf and made off with his money and jewelry. But John's safe."

The man in the blue ski sweater stepped up to Mrs. Whitman. "It was some slick dude with a salt and pepper beard. He's been working the ski lodges up here. It's a goldmine for thieves."

The next morning a small wrapped parcel was found under the large evergreen tree in the lobby of the lodge. It was addressed to John Whitman. It contained a handful of credit cards, a gold watch, and a diamond ring. A note was attached. It said: *Merry Christmas. Nick.*

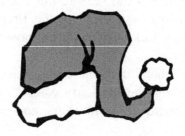

"IN THE NICK OF TIME" ORIGINALLY PUBLISHED BY WOLFMONT PRESS
IN *DYING IN A WINTER WONDERLAND* IN 2008.

A Role to Die For

I couldn't believe they found Brad's body. I thought I buried him deeper.

But eight years is a long time and a girl can forget little things like that. You know, stuff like: Where'd I park the car? Where'd I leave my shoes? Where'd I bury my boyfriend?

I knew where I buried him, just not how deep. Deeper's better. Trust me. Anyway, the first time you kill somebody is always trial and error.

By the second one, I had improved my technique.

And number three was... sheer perfection.

As for Brad... Dear Brad. Dear no-talented Brad Kingston who schmoozed the director into cutting my part down to a walk-on, he had it coming.

He wanted cutting. I showed him cutting. And not that little nip/tuck he got when he grew that second chin after scarfing down too much designer pizza.

Brad wanted to break it to me gently up at my cabin. How did he put it? A quiet little weekend where we can really get to know each other. Yeah, right. I learned he was a rat and he learned I had a temper.

We had been seeing each other since the cameras started rolling on the picture. Actors always fall in love with their co-stars, unless the co-star is a horse. Well, there was this one story...

Sorry, I digress.

As for Brad Kingston, he was a hand-me-down. I stole him from another actress, Barbara Sanders. We had been stealing choice men and even choicer roles from each other since we both starred in the same movie more than two decades earlier.

Brad was also gorgeous. He may have gotten top billing in the film, but I had been in the business longer, something he never let me forget. I played the "older woman" seduced by the lead character one steamy night.

I believe I seduced him the first time... that is, off camera. But his ego rewrote the scenario and it turned up in a snippet for *Variety* credited to "Unnamed Sources." The headline read: What Cinema Legend is putty in the hands of a certain Hollywood Heartthrob? Since there were only two of us at my house, I could do the math and figured out who was the "unnamed source" and who was "the putty."

We drove up to my place late that Friday afternoon so he could explain why I was getting the shaft. I actually started out with three more lines than Brad did in the movie. By the time they finished hacking up my part, I was lucky they didn't open the movie with my corpse being wheeled out of the room.

Brad walked into the cabin and plopped down on one of the long sofas. He unzipped his designer ski jacket and threw it on the floor.

"Come sit by me," he said, "after you take the luggage up to the bedroom. You know I'd offer to help, but I sprained my arm doing a stunt last week."

"I thought your stunt double hurt his arm."

"Well, yeah, but I have to let everybody think it was me. You know the old Hollywood image thing. But a little exercise is good for you. Not that you're fat or anything, but have you seen some of the girls on the set? I mean they're built like boys, except for the implants. You don't have implants, do you, Paula?"

"No, Brad. This is all me."

I didn't mention the face lift. Technically it was still my face, just the bags removed. And the tummy tuck and fanny lift. Those were subtractions, not additions. But no silicone.

"You come across great on camera," he said. "Even in the close-ups. But you know what?"

Okay. Here it comes. The boot.

"Your part might give you too much exposure. You wouldn't want that. Where's the mystery? But… If we trimmed off a few lines, tightened up those scenes so when the audience sees you, it'll be like dessert, something they crave, but something they shouldn't have too much of. Get it?"

"Yeah. Like pizza. Sure. Too much and you bloat."

He patted his repackaged chin and then changed the subject. "Where's the bar?"

He sprang off the sofa and rummaged through the cabinets while I toted the luggage. He was too busy looking for my good vodka to realize I left my things in the car.

This was my retreat in the mountains above Los Angeles, paid for by my long career in Hollywood. I started out doing ingénue parts and graduated to female leads. Groping and pawing went with getting bigger parts, but after a while I realized I could parlay my tangible assets into viable commodities. Diamonds really are a girl's best friend.

I stopped at the landing and watched the little creep scurrying around my place. I starred with better actors than this jerk when I was younger than he is, yet he thought he was so hot just because he had a TV series. Television! Bastard child of both the stage and film.

"Did you know Valentino?" he called after me, knowing the silent film star died three decades before I was born.

"Yeah. He was better in the sack than you, Brad."

That got him. He slammed down his unfilled glass and climbed the stairs after me. He had that sly look in his eye that said he was only half mad. I had him beat by fifty percent. I was 100% pissed.

I had tossed his luggage on the bedroom floor. He probably expected me to hang up his clothes and fold his socks. Ha!

"What's with the plastic tarp on the floor?" he said. "Are we gonna play Slip and Slide into bed?"

He brushed back his inky black hair and gave me a killer grin. I reached over and slit his throat.

What a mess. That's why I put down the tarp.

The knife was one of those $19.95 Ginsus they used to advertise on TV. Cuts a tomato so thin you could read the obituaries through it, or something like that.

Well. It didn't cut through everything. It sort of lodged between one of the soup bones at the back of his neck. Biology wasn't my best subject in high school, so I can't remember what it was called. But I couldn't cut through it.

Brad fell where he stood. But my beautiful blue ski sweater was ruined. Damn. I bought it while filming a movie in Aspen fifteen years ago. It still fit. And Brad said I needed exercise.

I got all the exercise I needed rolling his body up in that tarp and dragging it down the stairs. But I was even happier it was still cool up in the mountains. I hate to sweat and all this exertion was making me perspire.

I tugged off the bloody sweater. At forty-five, I still looked pretty good in a tank top and no bra. My personal trainer made sure the only chin I had was still taut. We were concentrating on those inner thighs. They still needed work.

Brad's firm, young body banged down the stairs with unpleasant thumps. I should put down a runner. The cabin might be rustic pine, but a little carpet on the steps wouldn't change the overall look of the place.

That's when I heard a car coming up the gravel drive.

Oh, no.

I wasn't dressed for company.

I pulled the tarp over to the hallway leading to the kitchen and straightened my hair. I could tell in the amber light from the deer antler chandelier I needed to touch up those black roots. I was known for my blonde hair and blonde it was going to stay.

The knock came.

I peered through the front curtains and saw the flashing red lights. This couldn't be good. Maybe there was a car accident down the mountain.

I opened the door to a handsome young sheriff's deputy not much older than Brad. His hair was lighter and his eyes were sky blue. Brad's were... Gee. What color were Brad's eyes?

"Is there a problem?" I asked.

He stared at me. I wondered if I had something caught between my teeth. I ran my tongue across my pearly whites, but didn't feel anything.

"Your car door's open," he said in an authoritative voice. "You'll run down your battery." Then he smiled. "You're Paula Douglas, aren't you?" His voice softened. "Gosh. I knew you lived up here. I hoped I'd have the chance to see you in person. I've seen every movie you ever made, twice."

"My car door?" I questioned.

"Uh...Yeah. I saw the dome light."

"Saw it from where?"

"Uh...as I drove up."

He was getting flustered. I like that in men.

"Do you usually go around checking people's dome lights?"

"No, ma'am... No, Miss Douglas... Ms. Douglas. Mountain lions."

"I beg your pardon?"

"They've spotted mountain lions in the area and we're warning residents to watch out."

"Mountain lions. How interesting."

And how convenient, I thought.

"Are you up here alone?" he asked.

"No. My... friend and I are spending the weekend."

"Brad Kingston. Sure. I read the papers. Is he here?" He looked over my shoulder.

"Cooling off... in the shower. We were bringing in the luggage and got carried away." I gave him a sexy grin and pumped the front of my tank top to let a little steam off. "If he weren't here I'd ask you in for a drink."

He blushed. "Can I help with the rest of the suitcases?"

"Sure. Just put them near the stairs. You're a doll."

"No problem, Ms. Douglas."

"Call me Paula."

He turned even redder and went outside for the bags. He set them near the stairs and then looked around the large room.

"What's that?" he asked, pointing to the tarp.

"Old rugs. I'm going to put new ones down so my toes don't get cold in the winter."

"Want me to haul it outside?" He stepped over to the roll.

I placed my hand on his arm. "The carpet people said not to let it get wet. Mold, you know."

"Oh, sure. Well, watch out for mountain lions."

"I'll do that."

"Gosh. I can't believe I really got to meet you." He sighed.

The cute deputy left.

An hour later I got Brad back in his ski jacket, dragged the tarp into my car, and drove it to a remote area several miles from my cabin. I spent an hour and a half digging my little heart out. I brought the vodka to make the job go easier. I dumped Brad into the hole, jammed the empty bottle in his jacket pocket, and covered him up. I swept leaves and twigs over the spot so it didn't look so fresh, and then drove another mile and stuffed the tarp and my beautiful sweater in a dumpster at a building site. I tossed more stones and concrete on top.

Then I drove home and took a shower. The next day I went down to the local store and bought steaks, a bottle of red wine, and some Brussels sprouts, Brad's favorite, or so said one of those slick movie magazines with his picture grinning from the cover last summer. There's another reason I don't like Brad. Nobody likes Brussels sprouts.

I called the carpet store later Saturday morning and asked them to install runners down the front stairs and a new carpet in the dining room. I yanked up two old rugs and rolled them up in another blue tarp and set it in the hallway so they could be carted off with the unused bits and pieces when the carpet people finished up on Monday.

At four o'clock Sunday afternoon I was buying more steak and Brussels sprouts at the market. I made sure to mention Brad was out walking in the woods.

"I hope he doesn't run into that mountain lion," said the obliging clerk who was stuffing the food into a canvas bag.

Clutching the collar of my gorgeous maroon parka, I said, "God, I hope not. Brad does all his own stunts, you know. It would be just like him to try and outsmart something tougher than he is."

By nine o'clock that evening the Sheriff and his cute deputy were in my living room. I did a scene worthy of Shakespeare showing fear and remorse for not begging Dear Brad the Adventurer to stay inside.

I saw the Sheriff poking around the tarp, but all it contained were those old rugs. Dinner sat untouched and growing cold on the dining room table. The candles had burned down to a nub. I hadn't even tried the wine. I would later. Me and the deputy. He was such a comfort.

I seldom visited the cabin above Los Angeles after that. Everybody understood. The memory of Brad must have been too much for me, people thought. I threw myself into my work. Miraculously, my part in the picture was increased. I had to fill yet another hole made by Brad Kingston.

But I rose to the challenge. I worked like a demon, studying and rewriting my lines until I got top billing and poor dead Brad got "In his final appearance" status. They had to use his stunt double in some of the remaining scenes. He was better than Brad ever was, especially in bed. I hope his career does well.

My next film was a tear jerker. Great wads of political correctness packed into a 92-minute script. It had Oscar written all over it.

Then "she" stepped on the set. She was as much a blonde as I was. I'd seen her sneak in the backdoor at Maxwell's on Rodeo Drive to get her roots touched up on occasion. I was leaving one time and took her taxi. The driver said she didn't leave a tip. I gave him one: Don't pick her up again.

She called herself Gwen Gentry. I doubt it was her real name. She looked like one of those cheap French dolls you'd win at the county fair. All ruffles, stringy hair, and puffy lips that didn't look so much "bee stinged" as punched in the puss. But men fell at her twenty-something feet. Every word out of her mouth was a pearl… before swine.

We had three big scenes together. I played her mother. What a piece of miscasting that was. I'd never give birth to that spawn from hell. She had a nasty little habit of whispering all her lines. It forced the director to bring the camera closer to her bird-like face so he could catch every breathy word. As the camera got closer, I got pushed farther away until I could have phoned in my lines.

"I just can't scream these wonderful words," Gwen twittered. "They're just too important to the scene. I must kiss them into the camera."

She closed the sale by leaning over the director, her silicone assets damn near dragging on his knees. "You…" she said to me with a wave of her boney hand. "Stand behind the camera. I'll deliver my lines by just imagining you're in front of me."

And she did. As if I were there, which I wasn't. I went back to my trailer and sulked.

When they called me for my next scene, the Moon Princess was sitting in her chair, her toadies groveling at her feet. I could hear Harry, the director, making a total fool out of himself as I approached.

"You are absolutely magnificent, Gwen," he drooled. "You absolutely light up the set."

I was "absolutely" going to puke.

But it got worse. Gwen wanted to be the only one on the screen. They could shoot over my shoulder or over my dead body, but she didn't want me in any shot with her.

"But Harry," she cooed. "Her coloring is so… odd. Look at that lipstick. And her skin tone." She turned to me and draped the lime green sleeve of her flowing gown over my head. "It's practically the same color. One of them has to go. And this dress really shows off my best features." She waggled her assets in his face.

"Paula," Harry said to me. "Why don't you sit in that wingback chair? We'll shoot just to the right of it and catch Gwen as she comes into the room. You talk with your hand. You're mad at your daughter for staying out late. Really sell it. Okay?"

My talking hand said its lines while the camera rolled past me and got another close-up of Gwen as she over-acted.

Harry couldn't contain himself. "Cut. Print. That was absolutely sensational, Gwen." He rushed to her like she would start levitating any minute. "Stars absolutely shoot out of your fingertips and hair."

I had co-star status in this movie, but I was seeing my part slowly erode. This was one of the tricks my nemesis, Barbara Sanders, used to pull back in our glory days. That's when I remembered: the Moon Princess was a close friend of Babs.

I sat there quietly, while a germ of an idea started growing in my head.

Two days later Little Miss Sunshine went into her metal trailer. It was after lunch and everyone knew she always brushed her perfect set of caps after every meal. But nobody knew about the frayed electrical wire that was mysteriously caught under the pipes running to her metal sink. Talk about shooting stars. They said her trailer danced with electric arcs like a bad horror movie. If she had any hair left, it was probably those black roots.

I was swapping Hollywood war stories in the lunchroom with the rest of the cast when the fireworks broke out.

"What was that?" I shrieked, diving under a table.

"Harry must have gone over budget and the producer blew his top," said one of the cameramen.

We all stayed under the tables, eating our sandwiches and drinking tea until someone came in and gave us the all clear and the bad news about poor Gwen. When somebody asked, "How is she?" I wanted to yell out "extra crispy," but I bit my tongue.

The fire department declared it a terrible accident. I guess that's one way of looking at it.

Again I got top billing in the movie. Harry was replaced as director due to stress, and the picture got an Oscar nomination. Alas. It didn't win.

Eight years passed. Fewer scripts were coming my way. I was now considered a "classic actress." That meant I was over fifty and only suited for character roles or cameo bits. The latter usually meant I could be killed off in a drama or made fun of in a comedy. Ah, youth. Like you won't get old.

I was past the age to have a "young lover" in my life, unless I paid big bucks for some Chippendale hunk to come over and take pity on me. For two-hundred dollars an hour they could fake enough pity for a run of *Les Miserables*.

Lots of middle-aged gals haunted trendy bars, picking up younger guys. There was even this hot new book out subtitled: *Cougar: A Guide for Older Women Dating Younger Men*, that was their bible. I read it… strictly out of curiosity, of course.

But what I wanted most was one more great role before I started doing "character" parts. Then I noticed an article in *Variety*.

It was late autumn and I was sitting in the backyard of my house up in the Hollywood Hills. The piece was about a book being optioned by the studios. I had actually read that one, too. I had a lot of time on my hands.

The book was *Cora's Secret*. It was one of those sagas about a bunch of women in a small town where everybody was sleeping with everybody else, and all the people knew everybody's business and innermost thoughts. All except this character called Cora. She was an enigma. She wandered into town a dozen years earlier and started a beauty parlor and handed out Ann Landers-type advice by the bucketful.

Cora was in her fifties and had this long scar along her cheekbone. Boy, that scar caused all kinds of talk around town. The gossip was rampant until somebody turned up dead. Then the story really took off.

The description of Cora fit me like a glove – right age group, right hair color, right body type. With make-up and lighting I could start out looking thirty in the flashbacks and gracefully age to mid-fifties. I had the dark roots, if I skipped a few sessions at Maxwell's. And I had the attitude – tough but introspective. I had to look that word up, but I had it up the ying yang.

I wanted that part.

I called my agent.

"Hey, Paula. What's up, babe?"

"Morrie, did you read the article in *Variety* about them optioning *Cora's Secret*?"

"Sure. It's the hottest property in town. Every starlet in Hollywood would kill for a part in that blockbuster."

"What about the part of Cora? Any names mentioned?"

"A few names have popped up," he said. "If Streep lost twenty pounds, she'd have it in a heart beat."

"I don't need to lose weight, Morrie. I'm the right size, right age. And my roots are already black. What do they want me to do, run a razorblade across my face?"

"Okay, Paula," he said with some hesitation. "I'll make a few calls."

I didn't hear from Morrie for over a week. That usually meant bad news. Then one rainy afternoon the phone rang.

"Hey, Paula. It's Morrie." His voice was shaking. "Are you sober?"

I looked at the clock. It was two in the afternoon. I put down my half empty martini glass. "Sober as a judge, Morrie."

"Are you sitting down?"

"I'm prostrate."

"Tell him to leave. I've got news."

"I'm alone, Morrie. What's the problem?"

"You got it," he said.

"I don't have anything catching," I said, misunderstanding his initial statement.

"No. You got the part. You got Cora."

My head started to spin. It had to be the alcohol. It had finally fried my brain. I hung up the phone, thinking I was hallucinating. It rang seconds later. It was Morrie.

"Hi, Morrie. I had the wildest dream."

"It's no dream, Paula. They want you for the part of Cora. I didn't even have to grovel. You were their first choice. After your two co-stars died in those movies you did a while back, they thought you already had a built-in tragic quality."

"Tragic?" I questioned before draining the martini glass and realizing what he meant. "Of course it was tragic. I lost…Uh…"

"Brad," he prompted.

"Yes, Brad, and then… the Princess. It was practically *Macbeth*. But you said they want me for Cora?"

"Yes. Come down to the studio. The place is buzzing with the news. They want you on *Larry King* tonight. You're not drinking, are you?"

"I'm a veritable Supreme Court Justice. I'll be there in less than an hour."

"I'll let everybody know," said Morrie. He was laughing like an idiot. Good old Morrie.

I grabbed the vodka bottle and stumbled into the bedroom where I happened to get a look at myself in the full length mirror. Whoa. The new set of bags under my eyes were perfect. And the black roots divine. I'll be terrific as Cora. I drank a toast to my middle-aged self.

I took a hot shower and then slipped into a bright red dress that did great things for my figure. I tried to get my toes into a pair of high heel shoes, but the shoes must have shrunk since the last time I put them on.

But that was good. Cora would never wear high heels. Only flats for her. But the dress was pure Cora. Tight in all the right places and a little short for her age. The author described her right down to the jingly bracelets on her wrists.

I dug through my junk jewelry drawer and brought out half a dozen cheap metal bracelets that clanged together beautifully. I even had a big beaded necklace that clashed with my dress. Yep. I had Cora down to a "T."

I scooped up my purse and ran out the front door. I had forgotten to put on lipstick, but I knew I had a particularly shocking shade of red in my bag. Once in the garage, I set my purse on the hood of the car and fumbled around for that tube of Molten Red lipstick.

Then a noise got my attention. It was a click, clickity, click. The second I recognized the sound, something struck me on the head and I went nighty-night.

I woke up coughing my lungs out. Something was over my mouth and I tried to yank it off.

"Keep it in place, Ms. Douglas. It's oxygen," said a voice coming out of the fog my head was in.

I blinked several times until a face came into view.

"Who are you?" I asked, but it came out, "Boo rar roo?"

The young man in green medical scrubs must speak that language, because he answered, "I'm a medic. You're in an ambulance."

The next thing I remembered was being wheeled down a cold corridor toward a bright light.

This can't be right. I'm sure I'll be going where the temperature is a whole lot hotter when I finally shuffle off this mortal coil.

Doors opened and I was rolled inside.

Men in white stared down at me. I snuck a quick look to see if I was bare assed, but a sheet covered all the X-Rated stuff. I still had the thing over my face, but my eyes were clear.

"How do you feel, Ms. Douglas?" said someone.

"Rawffull," I mumbled.

"You'll be fine. We just want to keep oxygen flowing to clean out your lungs. You had a nasty accident."

All the men in white did a double take like they had a great big secret.

"Wa happen?" I burbled.

"Exhaust fumes built up in your garage. If it wasn't for one of your neighbors, well, it might not have been a happy ending."

Oh, crap. Now I'd have to be nice to all my neighbors until I find out who the Good Samaritan was. Never mind. I decided to worry about that later.

The doctors looked me over good before they took me upstairs to a private room.

That's when I noticed a shadow pass by the door a few times. Finally it stopped. Uh oh. It's the Grim Reaper. I'm outta here.

I heard heavy shoes clomp nearer. Of course my Grim Reaper would sound like a Clydesdale.

"Who's there?" I said, my voice much stronger than I thought I was.

"It's me, Paula," came the timid reply.

"Morrie? What are you doing out in the hall?"

He peeked inside. His face was tofu white and his eyes were two large black olives. "How do you feel?" he said.

"Like I was strapped behind a city bus for eight hours. How are you?"

"Not so good." He stumbled into the room and plopped down in the only chair. He wiped his forehead with his sleeve and panted like a rabid dog.

"You need to calm down there, Morrie." I reached over and patted his hand. I handed him my glass of water and he drank.

"I'm so… so glad you're still alive," he stuttered, spitting water across the sheets.

"Yeah. Me, too."

"Why?" he said, his head nearly between his knees.

"Because I'd rather be alive than dead?" I suggested, hoping my answer would clear his mind. And here I thought I was the one in a daze.

"No. Why'd you try to kill yourself?"

"What?" I shrieked. "Who are you talking to, Morrie? It's me. Paula. You know. The actress. Your client."

His little head bobbed up. "You mean you didn't…? Oh, God, Paula. I knew you'd never kill yourself. Maybe somebody else… but never yourself."

I let that last remark pass. "Who thinks I tried bumping myself off?"

He looked at the TV over my head. "Everybody."

So that's why the quacks were laughing up their white sleeves. I could still feel the lump on my head. Did they think I bashed myself and then sucked the exhaust?

My doctor strolled in later that evening after Morrie had left. He smelled like rubbing alcohol and linguini sauce. I would have preferred what he had for dinner than the gruel I was offered. I eyed the phone and wondered if Red Lobster would deliver to a hospital room.

"How are we feeling, Ms. Douglas?"

"We feel terrif, doc. Did you notice the bump on my head?"

"We X-rayed it and it doesn't look like there is any permanent damage," he said. "Does it hurt?"

"No. But who's saying I tried to kill myself?"

He glanced at the TV hanging on the wall.

"Since when does the boob tube make medical diagnoses?" I asked.

"I'll be happy to make a statement to the media on your behalf, Ms. Douglas, but it might be a little late."

He picked up the remote and switched to a local news channel. We didn't have to wait through ten commercials or endure the weather report. There I was behind the announcer, or at least a picture of me from one of my earlier movies when I played a drug addict. I never liked that movie.

The wardrobe wasn't worth stealing. The reporter could have picked one where I looked better. But the storyline required me at my worst.

"...found near death in her garage this afternoon," the reporter was saying. "Unnamed sources say she was dreading going back to work after so many years due to her age and physical condition and she tried to take her own life. Friends of the well-known actress have rallied around the one-time beauty of stage and screen."

The picture switched to a tacky living room setting. It looked like something out of *A Streetcar Named Desire*. I didn't know anybody who lived in a dump like that, and frankly, I didn't know anybody who knew me well enough to know what I was thinking. The news cam scanned the scene and that's when I saw the theater seats out front. It was a stage setting. And it was *Streetcar*. I had auditioned for the role of Blanche Dubois at the Ahmanson Theater earlier in the year, but somebody sabotaged my chances. I ate myself nearly into oblivion after losing the part.

Then I heard a sound. Click clickity click. Someone was walking across the stage toward the reporter and her cameraman.

The hum of the medical equipment and the chatter of the television stopped. All I heard was the pounding of my heart and the click of those high heels.

On the screen was my nemesis, Barbara Sanders.

There's a joke around Hollywood: If Paula Douglas is too drunk for a part, Barbara Sanders will fill her shoes. The story originated with Barbara and everybody knew it, but this bitch had been dogging my trail my entire career. Whichever designer did my gown for the Oscars, she had a knock-off in a similar color. If I arrived in a Rolls Royce, she tooled up in a Bentley. And worst of all, any movie role I got, she wanted.

Now I knew what this was all about. Barbara wanted Cora. That cow wanted my part and tried to kill me.

I heard a distant voice calling my name. "Ms. Douglas! Ms. Douglas!"

Then someone slapped my face. I pulled back my fist and was going to slug the creep, but my eyes focused and I realized I was aiming at the doctor.

"Everything's Okay, Ms. Douglas. Take a little oxygen to clear your head."

While he put the mask over my mouth and turned the valve, my eyes floated back to the television screen. Barbara Sanders was still talking.

"…very good friend of mine. I've known her for ages, though she's much older than I am, of course. It's pitiful she tried something like this."

"Liar," I said, pulling off the mask.

"I know you didn't try to kill yourself, Ms. Douglas," said the doctor.

"No, that she's a friend of mine," I stated.

I put the oxygen mask back on and sucked down some O2. My head did clear. I knew exactly what I was going to do. They released me from the hospital the next day. I talked the doc into letting me take a portable canister of oxygen home in case I needed to refresh my lungs. Cough. Cough.

Five nights later I drove over to Barbara's house. I had been following her home from the theater for several nights. She pulled into her garage and I slipped in before she turned off the engine.

"Keep the motor running, sweetie." I aimed a gun in her surprised face. It was a prop gun I had liberated from one of the movies I had done, but I thought it would work if it had bullets. It didn't have any, but I was sure Babs wouldn't know that. "Punch the button for the garage door," I added, and she obeyed.

"You must be crazy," she said.

"A cliché if I ever heard one. Of course I'm crazy, and pissed, and a few other things."

"What do you want?" she asked.

"Another cliché," I said. "Who writes your dialogue?"

"What are you talking about?"

She tried to open the car door.

I pushed it closed with my knee. "Sit."

Her pudgy face looked up at me. She no more looked like Blanche Dubois than I did. But she did look like Cora. Even her roots were dark. I climbed in the back seat with my bag and rolled down the window.

"Ah, nothing like a ride in the country. Huh, Barbara?"

"You won't get away with this," she said.

"And you won't get Cora," I said.

"How did you know I—"

"I know you, sweetie. Just keep breathing in that fresh air."

She swiveled in her seat and stared at me. I touched the barrel of the gun to her redesigned nose.

"Turn around and just listen," I said.

Barbara sat back in her seat and glared at me in the rearview mirror.

"Flip the mirror so I don't have to look at you," I said.

She gave a little cough and obeyed. Exhaust fumes were getting thicker in the closed garage.

I stared at her black roots and said, "You sent your discarded boyfriend over to me knowing he'd use me just like he used you. Brant—"

"Brad," she corrected, her head lolling back against the head rest.

"Whatever. He used me and was going to have my part cut down to a cameo. Was that your idea? Don't answer. And then came the Moon Princess. She was your friend. I should have recognized the signs. You have thrown monkey wrenches into my career from day one. How many producers did you sleep with just so you could screw me?"

Her coughs were deeper now.

"But Cora... The studio gave the part to me...To *me*." I hit the headrest with the gun. "Morrie didn't have to bribe or blackmail anybody. I got it because it was made for me."

I reached into my bag and pulled out the gas mask and took a few gulps of clean air from the portable canister.

"I *am* Cora," I said. "The lady with a past and a future. But not you, sweetie."

I kept the mask over my mouth until I saw Barbara slump in the seat. I got out of the car, retrieved my bag, opened the side door in the garage, still wearing the plastic gloves I had taken from the hospital, and walked back to my car. The street was deserted.

I drove down one of the main drags in town when all of a sudden saw something. I slammed on my brakes.

Taco Bell! I was starving. I pulled into their drive-through and ordered a large burrito and a coke. I got home before one o'clock, took a shower, and hit the sack.

That was over three months ago. I was already running my lines for the part in *Cora's Secret*. The publicity for the upcoming movie was awesome. I was wined, dined, and interviewed. Somebody even asked me about Barbara's suicide. It was assumed she killed herself because she didn't get the part. I nodded along.

"Did you go to her funeral?" asked the interviewer.

"Sad to say, no. I had a prior engagement." I had to reline my lingerie drawers. A girl does have her priorities.

I had a free weekend coming up and decided to go to the cabin. It had been years since I spent any quality time there. I noticed all the new construction in town. The quaint village was getting un-quaint. Burger places were edging out the vine covered eateries, and two new hotels bookended main street. I thought about selling my place.

I dropped my luggage in the entryway and made myself a drink. It had been a long drive.

There was a knock on my door.

Drat. Neighbors.

I peeked through the curtain and saw the car. My heart skipped a beat. It was my cute deputy. I hadn't seen him since that one fantastic evening, but I thought of him often. He was the only person in my entire life who treated me like a woman, not a movie star.

"Hello, Paula," he said when I opened the door, his blue eyes as bright as ever. His uniform seemed different. He didn't look like Smokey the Bear anymore, but he did look hot. I started thinking about those older women lusting after younger men.

"Aaron. How did you know I was back?" I asked.

"I drive by your place every now and then, just to check it out."

"New uniform?"

"Promotion. I'm sheriff now."

"Congratulations." I noticed he had a plastic bag clutched in his hand. "Want to come in for a drink?"

"I'm on duty. We found Kingston's body," he said in his next breath.

I had to think a minute before remembering who that was. "Poor Brant...Brad," I corrected myself.

"They were excavating for a new motel down the road and uncovered his remains."

"I'm surprised they could identify him after all these years," I said.

"His credit cards were still intact. So was this." He pulled a vodka bottle out of the plastic bag. "Didn't you say he was drinking the day he disappeared?"

I didn't remember, but it sounded good to me. "Yes. I'm sure he had a few drinks to keep warm on his walk."

"The bottle was in an inside pocket of his jacket. The waterproofing kept it in almost pristine condition."

"The marvels of modern science," I said.

"I've been following your career," Aaron said, changing the subject. "I have every biography ever written about you. You had it rough in Hollywood. Lots of backstabbing."

"It was like a long run of *Julius Caesar*. But you grow a thick skin, if you want to survive."

"Some of the things done to you must have left scars," he said.

"I have a few."

"I read about your miscarriage on the set with that awful actress who recently killed herself. I wish I could have been there for you."

"I try to forget, but I don't always take my own advice."

"You gave me some advice, Paula," said Aaron, his voice soft and comforting. "Remember when I stayed here that one night?"

"Sure." It was as close as I'll ever get to heaven, I thought.

"You told me to go for my dream. I did, and made sheriff."

"It's great to have a dream," I said, looking at the script for *Cora's Secret* on the table.

He was still holding the vodka bottle. It was the good Grey Goose.

"Brant's—" he started to say.

"Brad," I corrected.

"Brad's fingerprints weren't on the bottle. Just yours."

"Sure I couldn't offer you a drink? I have more vodka."

"Still on duty." He studied me with those blue eyes. "The coroner examined the remains. There wasn't much left. The body must have been hastily buried and years of using the site as a local dump covered it even more."

"Hastily buried?" I questioned, remembering the hour and a half I sweated over that hole.

"They think an animal killed him, dug a shallow trench to hide his kill for later, and must have forgotten where it was buried." He walked closer and put his warm hand on my arm. "It was ruled…death by cougar."

Aaron smashed the plastic bag containing the vodka bottle against the fireplace and the glass shattered. Then he took my hand and led me upstairs.

I'll always wonder if he ever read that "cougar" book, but I'll never ask. Lovers have to have some secrets.

"A Role to Die For" originally published by Spygame Press in *From Light **To Dark**,* in 2012.

There is a burden that goes with the badge. Sometimes it's heavier than we care to admit.

Heat

It was going to be the hottest damn day of the year. Those Santa Anas were kicking up, turning the L.A. basin into a blast furnace. If it didn't cool off, half the state would catch fire.

I was cruising along Sunset when the A.P.B. went out. Shots fired. They called the coroner, too. I hooked a U, headed toward the crime scene, and was just a block away when the dispatcher got around to the description of the suspect.

The owner of a shoe repair shop next to the convenience store phoned in the alarm. He had hunkered down behind his counter, afraid to look out the window, but when he finally stood up, he saw a black man wearing a dark green T-shirt running from the scene carrying a large yellow sack.

I spotted a guy in a green shirt sprinting down the street with a bright yellow bag under his arm. I pulled the black & white to the curb and took off on foot. There wasn't another soul out in that oven except the dim-witted suspect and a shmuck with a badge.

Within half a block I was sweating like a pig. My eyes stung from the brine dripping down my face. I wiped it away with my sleeve. When I looked again, the man had vanished. I figured he went down an alley. I took a shortcut between a taco joint and a newspaper stand and found myself in a deserted alleyway. I heard footsteps and headed toward them.

The guy must have been a ghost, because I could hear him, but I couldn't see him. I went a few more blocks dodging crates and broken bottles. That's when I noticed the yellow bag on the ground. It was a bag of birdseed. Who the hell kills somebody over a bag of birdseed?

I kept running.

My size twelve shoes slapped against the hot pavement. I stopped to listen for any movement. A faint rustle caught my attention. The man in the green T-shirt darted out of a doorway, stopped, and looked directly at me, and then took off.

I heaved a sigh and started after him. I knew I'd catch him, if not on the street, at his apartment. I recognized the bum. I'd done this before.

We ran along another street, but he was a good thirty feet ahead of me. He reached one of the main drags and raced down the middle of the busy thoroughfare. Horns honked and tires screeched as he cut between vehicles and continued his mad dash into that new neighborhood. The sight of my uniform stopped some of the cars, but most of them kept coming. It was too hot to worry about two maniacs on foot. That's when I dodged a laundry truck, while he ducked into a Chinese restaurant. I followed.

The place was packed with people eating steamed rice and noodles even on a hot day like that. I don't think the air conditioning was working. The patrons kept their heads down, studying the few bits of rice pinched between their chopsticks. A black man running and a white cop yelling were invisible in Chinatown.

I looked around, but didn't see him in the dining room. I made for the kitchen.

The cooks and the assorted help were already plastered against the walls, cleavers, spoons, and bowls in hand. Nobody said a word. They held their breaths. I held my gun.

Then I heard it. Slam! A screen door closed in a storeroom off the kitchen. I left them to their egg foo yong and dashed into the dimly lit room, dropping into a crouch just in case my quarry was smart enough to fake me out. Nobody shot back, so I went to the rear door, kicked it open, waited for bullets to blow more holes in the screen, and then did another duck and run into the alley.

The area was thick with flies. I wanted to fire off a few warning shots just to get them out of my face. I swatted the swarm away and realized I was pumping sour air up my nose. It smelled like week-old takeout. I spat a bug out of my mouth and ran a few more yards.

I heard commotion nearby. Voices. I couldn't make out a word they were saying. I sprinted down the alley and onto another sidewalk. The sounds came from the next street. I jogged to the narrow access and saw them standing there, arguing. An old woman wearing thick black stockings had him by the sleeve, howling at him in Chinese. She was two feet shorter, but she held onto him like a Pit Bull.

"Don't move, T-Bone. Or I'll shoot," I ordered.

He turned in slow motion. "Whatchew talkin' 'bout? I ain't movin'."

"Drop the gun!"

The woman started hitting him with her fists. She punched away until he gave her a shove like a pissed off hockey player. The old bat screamed all the way to the ground, but she jumped to her feet so fast I couldn't get off a clear shot, even if I wanted to. She followed him down the alleyway waving her fist and cursing. I had to damn near throw her against the wall to get her out of my way. By the time I got past her, T-Bone had pulled another disappearing act.

Two blocks further on, I found myself on a different street in Chinatown. This wasn't my beat and I really didn't want to be there. I hated the smell of dead fish. I hated the stench of rotting chicken. I hated the endless heat.

That's when I felt it. The tug on my holster. My gun wasn't in it, but I jumped a foot and spun around.

Nothing was there.

I heard a voice.

I glanced around and then looked down.

He was just over three-feet tall and grinning like an idiot. My gun brushed over his jet-black hair. I jerked the weapon away before I blew off the top of his head. He smiled at me like he knew me, but I didn't know anybody in that division, especially a small fry like that. The only Chinese kid…

He pointed frantically. Up. Up to the sky. I saw the shadow. It loped along the roof.

T-Bone.

I looked around for a fire escape. Nothing. I couldn't even find a doorway. It was like they evaporated. The street had turned into one long concrete channel. The only thing left was the overwhelming smell of dead fish.

"How did he get up there?" I said more to myself than to my snitch.

The boy pointed again. He took my arm and dragged me around a corner and I saw it. A fire escape. The metal ladder hadn't been pulled all the way down.

T-Bone must be in better shape than I thought. He outweighed me by twenty pounds, but I carried about that much in body armor and bullets. So I guess it was an even match. And the guy had to be pushing fifty. I was six years younger, but lately I didn't think I was in shape for anything tougher than pounding the pavement, especially in this heat. My legs already felt like they were slogging through quicksand.

I holstered my service revolver and grabbed for the bottom rung. It was stuck. Damn. I went back a couple of steps and then ran a few feet and jumped. I seized the second rung, but as I tried to haul my weight up the ladder, the catch gave way and the ladder slid with me on it to the ground. The little guy was standing right next to me, laughing. He must have been eating some sticky, red candy, because he had it smeared all over his face and hands. But he was still smiling and pointing up.

"Thanks, kid. I get it now. I'm supposed to go up, not fall on my butt."

"My name Kim. What your name?"

"Jack."

"Kim. Jack. Kim. Jack. Ha, ha, ha, ha."

I got to my feet and started to scale the metal ladder. I was going to tell the kid to stay where he was, but when I glanced down he had vanished. He must have dropped his candy and it melted, because all that remained was a large red splotch.

I climbed to the top of the ladder and looked around. I blew out a long, hot breath. I swear I'd been on that roof before. I remembered the forest of TV antennas crowding one corner of the building. And the sign for Lucky Cat Soy Sauce. Yeah. I know it was the same sign. But then there must be a million signs for soy sauce all over Los Angeles.

It was ten degrees hotter up there. Black tar oozed from under what was left of the tarpaper that covered the flat roof. My shoes stuck to the inky globs and they made a sucking sound when I moved. But I wasn't moving much. I was listening. Listening for any sound that would tell me where he was.

All I could hear was the traffic groaning up Hill Street as people tried to get off the egg-frying street and into some shade. Horns honked, hot horns like Wynton Marsalis. But these had an edge. One that said: If you slow down I'll ram this car up your tail pipe. Hurry up. Run the light. Get out of this blasted heat.

Even the birds stayed away, afraid they'd get those tiny feet caught in all that black ooze.

I was breathing hard by then. I had chased the guy on foot for a dozen blocks and was gasping for whatever air I could find hanging around on that flat roof. A whole host of heat apparitions waved at me as they clawed their way to heaven. I could see their bony fingers urging me to walk closer to the edge. I pulled my automatic and checked out the area. Other than those antennas and apparitions, I was alone. Oh, yeah. The smiling cat was still there.

I heard the rumble of an air conditioning unit in a small louvered shed. It did its best to push more hot air into my face. I tried the door to the little room. It was locked. Who locks up hot air?

I stopped to listen for T-Bone. I couldn't hear anything but the air conditioner. He must have stopped and was listening for me. Or maybe he had found a way down to the street and had slid onto a cool leather seat at the drugstore on the corner, and ordered a tall glass of ice tea. Man, I could go for that.

"T-Bone, you son-of-a-bitch. Where are you?"

"He probably wanted to get out of this heat, honey," said a soft voice.

I could just make out the pale blue dress on the other side of the air conditioning shed. She moved and it looked like somebody tore out a piece of the sky. She walked around to my side and cocked her head.

"Misty, you're not supposed to be up here. How'd you get on this roof?"

"The same way you did, Jack," she said in that baby doll voice of hers.

"Yeah, right. I'm sure you climbed that ladder in your muumuu."

"This is a designer dress. I got it half price at Marcel's."

"You got it off the back of a delivery truck after showing the driver a good time. Don't try to kid me, Misty."

"I'm not turning tricks anymore, Jack. You set me straight. Remember?"

"Yeah, and I remember you said you'd screw the undertaker if he promised to let you down easy. Come on. What do you want?"

"Just wanted to see how you were doing. Still on vice?"

"No. You saw to that."

"I didn't mean to. Is your wife glad you don't work nights anymore?"

"I don't think she much cares what I do."

"That's too bad, Jack. Like, I think you're a really cool guy. You've always been fair to me. She oughtta know ya like I do."

"She thinks I know you too well."

"But it's not true, Jack. You're just my friend."

"I don't think a woman like Helen would understand, Misty."

"She's crazy. You're a good man. You're the first guy I ever met who never tried anything with me."

"Is that right? You've had a rough life, kid. How old are you now?"

"Twenty-two."

"That's too young to have a rap sheet like yours, Misty."

"You've got a really big heart, Jack."

She dropped her head. I thought I saw her chin start to quiver. Big wet drops fell on her dress and started to spread across her chest. I hate it when women cry. I can never say the right thing. My wife said I shouldn't say anything at all because I just make things worse. She ought to know.

"I'm sorry if I made you cry, Misty. But it isn't safe for you up here. And I like your dress. Weren't you wearing it the last time I saw you? Did you get something on it? Is that nail polish?"

She wiped her hand over the fabric. "Oh, no. My beautiful dress. I don't wanna ruin my beautiful new dress. It's the only nice thing I have."

"Maybe we can find you another one. You remember the name of the driver who gave you the dress?"

"I'm a good girl now, Jack. I'm a real good girl. I don't do that anymore."

"What about Cool Ice? Is he gonna let you out of his stable when you're the hottest card in the deck?"

"Maybe like you could help me. Huh, Jack? You could like take him down for hustling us girls and like maybe you could put him in the joint for like a long time?"

"Didn't we try that already?"

"Did we? I don't remember. But watch out, Jack. They're after you."

"That's what you said the last time I saw you. Over at Mickey's Bar. But Tony and the boys were too hopped up on meth to see us coming. You remember how it went down. They were firing more lead at us than

Colombian drug lords. It was hot that day, too. You remember. In fact, I thought…

I looked around and she had disappeared. I guess I bored her with the story. I know I'd told her the same account a dozen times and she never stayed to hear it to the end. But I liked her dress. Except for the stains.

I heard a noise.

"Misty?"

"My name ain't Misty. You knows that, Jack."

"T-Bone. Where are you?"

"I'm up on diss here roof witch you, Jack."

"I'm getting too old for this, T-Bone. Aren't you getting a little tired?"

"Sure am. I thinks I be sittin' down for a spell."

"Hot, ain't it?"

"'Bout the hottest damn day I ever did see."

"That's what I was thinking."

"Hey, Mr. Jack. You got some water over there?"

"Yeah, T-Bone. I got plenty a water. And some ice. Come on out and have a big ol' glass of water with me. Hurry up before I drink it all myself."

"You ain't got no water, cop. I knows how you operate. You says you got water and whens I step out in front of y'all, you be blastin' me. I ain't dat stupid, man. You got any Moon Pies witch you?"

"No Moon Pies, T-Bone. You sittin' in the sun over there or maybe you found yourself some shade. It's so cool on this side of the building I just might catch pneumonia. How is it over on your side?"

"It ain't very cool over here. How comes it be cooler where you is?"

"I'm on the north side of the building. It's always chilly on the north side."

"You funnin' me? Why don't we change places for a while. I needs to cool off. I done sweat through my shirt and makin' a puddle right chere."

"No. I can't do that, T-Bone. I'd get written up for it. Aiding and abetting a fugitive they'd call it. But you could walk over here and we could talk for a while. Sound okay to you?"

"My memory ain't that good, but ain't that what you done tried the last time I got myself into this 'sitiation'?"

"Yeah, but we can get you help this time."

"That's what you cops always say, Mr. Jack. I don't think I been helped much."

"What do you want us to do?"

"Make them voices in my head go away."

"You have to keep taking your medication, T-Bone. That'll fix you up."

"Them don't help no mo'. I keeps hearin' them voices tellin' me to do stuff."

"Like kill that clerk?"

"Yeah 'cause he said I can't take what I needs."

"But T-Bone, you know you can't just take stuff 'cause you want it."

"I heard them voices say I could 'cause I be poor and they hads plenty."

"That's just a myth, T-Bone."

"A what?"

"A myth. It's a story people keep passing around 'til everybody starts believing it."

"Well it don't seem fair, do it? They gots plenty a stuff at the Seben-'Leven."

"You can't do it that way, T-Bone. If you come with me, I can get you set up in one of those homes I've been telling you about. They'll take good care of you. Treat you real nice and make sure you eat three times a day."

"I can do that now over at the mission. They done feed me a good dinner las' night and I don't got to go to the church lesson if'n I don't feels like it."

"Maybe we can get you in some place permanent. But you've got to come with me now."

"I ain't gonna do that, Mr. Jack. I gots to stay here and take care of the ones that needs me."

"Who needs you, T-Bone? You don't have any family."

"I have my chil'ren. I feeds dem."

"Children?"

"Sure 'nough. I's got plenty of chil'ren that I takes care of right chere at the lake."

"We're not in Echo Park, T-Bone. You ran about twelve blocks when I was chasing you."

"We ain't near the park? We gots to be. Who's gonna take care of my chil'ren if'n I ain't there?"

"Where do they stay? Your children. I never saw any kids at your place."

"They's there. Some a dem lives up on da roof like up here. I thoughts I was home. I rightly did."

"What do your children look like, T-Bone?"

I asked the question because I thought maybe T-Bone was hallucinating again. Sometimes he imagined he was one place when he was altogether somewhere else, like on another planet.

"Why they looks like me, they does. Just like me."

"T-Bone, why don't I drive you back to your place and you can show me those kids you got? Okay?"

"I don't know. Maybe they won't be there."

"Why wouldn't they be there?"

"Sometimes they just flies off. You knows how they be."

"We'll wait for 'em."

"If'n they don't show up, you be thinkin' I needs my medication."

T-Bone's voice was getting jerky. I had to change tactics.

"I won't think that. We'll just wait. Have some ice tea or something."

"Hold on, Mr. Jack. There be one up here now. I knew they'd find their ol' pappy."

I could hear T-Bone shuffling across the roof.

"You stay right there, boy," he said. "I be getting you—Don't you walk there! Now see what you done did."

"Dammit, T-Bone. It's hot up here. You don't have any kids. You need help."

"I'll show you, Mr. Jack! I'll show you!"

I heard his feet slapping over the flat roof. His shoes made loud sucking noises as he headed for me. The sun was to his back and I only saw the outline of the weapon. It was gray and heavy in his hand. He pointed it in my direction and I got off two shots. They hit him twice in the chest.

He kept coming. Suck. Suck. Suck. He slowed down as the tar grabbed the soles of his shoes and the bullets did their thing. He raised his hand again and I saw it clearly. I yanked my hand up and let the third shot sail into the sky. T-Bone's butterscotch-colored eyes swam with tears as he stood there, still holding the heavy object, then he dropped to his knees in front of me.

"They be my kids, Mr. Jack. I takes care of 'em. Diss one done got his feet caught in the tar on diss here roof. I save dem whens I can. Dats why I needs the birdseed."

He eased himself to the tarpaper floor and then went limp. His right hand was extended in my direction. I opened his fingers and retrieved the soft gray dove clutched in his fist. The bird's pink feet were caked with tar.

"Oh God, no. Not again." I shut my eyes.

I woke up sweating.

"Jack! Are you up yet? It's after eight."

There didn't seem to be any air in the room. I tried kicking off the sheets and looked at the alarm clock. I must not have set it.

"Jack?" said Helen, leaning into the bedroom. She was already dressed for work. "I left you one of those sausage-egg thingies in the micro. Don't let it go more than two minutes or the cheese turns to Napalm."

She looked at me knotted up in the sheet. She told me that was the reason she decided to sleep in the guest room. That and the sweating.

"Get any sleep?" she asked.

"Sure. Loads." I wiped the moisture from my upper lip.

She stared at me. "Was the Chinese boy in your dream?"

I threw my legs over the side of the bed and sat up. I rubbed my eyes.

"Yeah, but he was alive this time. Usually he isn't alive."

"Maybe that means you're getting better, Jack. Do you think that's what it means?"

"Maybe. T-Bone still got shot. And he still had the dove in his hand."

"Well, I think it means you're getting better. Isn't that what the police psychiatrist said?"

"She doesn't say much. I do most of the talking."

"Nobody blames you, Jack. The kid's death was an accident and it was a long time ago. And you didn't kill the prostitute. You should try to get over it. Everybody else has."

"Yeah."

"You going into work today?"

"Yeah."

"That's good, Jack. Call me at lunchtime."

"Sure."

"Gotta run or I'll miss my ride. And feed those damn birds of yours on the roof. I still don't know why you had to take them."

I heard the front door close as I walked into the bathroom. I didn't bother letting the shower run to get warm. It was going to be another hot day. Sometimes I think it's never gonna cool down. I stepped into the cold shower and let the water run down my back.

"God, that feels good."

I closed my eyes.

All I kept thinking was, I'd really like to go back to sleep.

I'd like to have that dream again.

I'd like to tell them I'm sorry.

"HEAT" ORIGINALLY PUBLISHED BY SPYGAME PRESS
IN *FROM LIGHT TO DARK* IN 2012.

POLICE LINE DO NOT CROSS

Author Bio

A former private detective and once a reporter for a small weekly newspaper, Gayle Bartos-Pool has numerous books in print: *Media Justice, Hedge Bet,* and *Damning Evidence* in the Gin Caulfield P.I. series; *The Johnny Casino Casebook 1- Past Imperfect; The Johnny Casino Casebook 2 – Looking for Johnny Nobody; The Johnny Casino Casebook 3 – Just Shoot Me; From Light To DARK*, a collection of short mystery stories; *Eddie Buick's Last Case; Enchanted – The Ring, The Rose and The Rapier; The Santa Claus Singer, Bearnard's Christmas, The Santa Claus Machine*, and The SPYGAME Trilogy – *The Odd Man, Dry Bones*, and *Star Power* and also *Caverns*. She is the former Speakers Bureau Director for Sisters-in-Crime/Los Angeles and a member of Mystery Writers of America. She teaches writing classes: "Anatomy of a Short Story," "How to Write Convincing Dialogue" and "Writing a Killer Opening Line" in sunny Southern California. Website: www.gbpool.com.

Most of the short stories referenced in this workbook can be found in *From Light To Dark* by G.B. Pool, published by SPYGAME Press. Other short stories by this author are in *The Johnny Casino Casebook* Series 1, 2, and 3 also published by SPYGAME Press. Books available on Amazon.com. Some references are from novels by G.B. Pool. The complete list of her books is in the front of this workbook.

Made in the USA
Coppell, TX
15 February 2020